D0138688

The Creation

HENRY HOLT AND COMPANY

# of Sculpture

JULES STRUPPECK

NEWCOMB COLLEGE SCHOOL OF ART

TULANE UNIVERSITY

PHOTOGRAPHS BY THE AUTHOR

New York

731
S 927

(CUD)
NB
1170
.S8X
1952

COPYRIGHT, 1952, BY HENRY HOLT AND COMPANY, INC.

LIBRARY OF CONGRESS CATALOG CARD NUMBER: 52-7020

PRINTED IN THE UNITED STATES OF AMERICA

WITHDRAWN

WEST BADEN COLLEGE
LIBRARY
122360

DESIGN BY JOHN KING

ACKNOWLEDGMENTS

I EXPRESS here my gratitude to all those who have helped in the development of this book, particularly to my students whose work has been the basis for the book.

Special acknowledgment must be given to: Miss Barbara Wedemeyer for her valuable assistance in the preparation of the manuscript; Mr. Robert D. Feild for his encouragement and guidance; Miss Edith Levy, Mr. Roy Trahan, and Mr. Armand Bertin for advice and assistance in making the photographs; Mr. Charles W. Ammen, Mr. Sampson J. Pitre, Jr., and Mr. Eugene Rouse for advice and assistance in metal casting; Mr. Owen H. Foss for advice on some of the technical problems; Mr. Robert G. Scott for valuable criticisms and suggestions during the preparation of the manuscript; Dr. Harold N. Lee for the painstaking care with which he checked the manuscript; and, finally, Mr. Duncan Ferguson whose penetrating and thorough criticisms of the manuscript resulted in some important changes which greatly improved the text.

New Orleans, La.   J. S.
January 7, 1952

CONTENTS

INTRODUCTION

ANY BOOK that deals with a subject as complex as the creative processes in sculpture needs a qualifying introduction.

Sculpture expresses itself in the only way sculpture can be expressed—visually. Discussions of sculpture are continually handicapped by the simple fact that sculptural concepts are not verbal but *visual* communications. If such concepts could be expressed adequately in words, it would not be necessary to manifest them in the much more difficult mediums of sculpture. The teacher of sculpture often wants to say just "Look!" when asked for specific verbal explanations. But this desire for a literal meaning indicates an obstruction in the mind of the questioner, and he cannot really profit from his visual experience until the obstruction is identified and then removed.

While it is impossible to explain sculpture verbally it *is* possible to free the student's mind of false ideas about what sculpture should be, and to help him discover basic considerations. The result can be real communication between sculpture and the student.

The Creation of Sculpture, in part, is devoted to the task of establishing bases from which individuals can find their own particular ways. These bases are, of course, greatly simplified—oversimplified in places, perhaps—but if taken as beginnings rather than as conclusions, they serve their purposes. While not given in conclusive detail, many of the arguments here will stimulate the ideas that come normally after considerable experience with sculpture. One alternative—making only guarded and qualified statements—would have led into a labyrinth of verbiage and prevented getting to the real problem of creating sculpture: learning through doing. Another alternative—the presentation of sculpture techniques—was rejected for two reasons. First, *The Creation of Sculpture* proposes to be more than a reference work; and second, it

viii

is a book opposed to the idea that technique can be separated from the creative process.

This book, therefore, is organized into a series of problems involving various technical means and demonstrating the functions of materials and techniques in the creative process. The first problems are simple studies in clay which enable the student to create from the beginning. They are flexible enough to tax abilities on any level. Each problem is designed to introduce at least one aspect of sculpture not already studied in previous problems. Consideration is given to the development of individual initiative, and as the problems advance the student is encouraged to develop his own discipline.

While the method and approach presented in this book have been found to be effective in practice, they are not presumed to be superior to all others. There are many ways of teaching sculpture. For instance, there is no reason to assume that one should begin with clay. It may be argued that clay is a more difficult medium than stone or wood and that one can best learn the rudiments of sculpture by carving. But regardless of the method, the teaching of sculpture is ultimately an individualized process. No book can replace the personal guidance of a competent teacher.

Those who wish to learn to produce sculpture but who are unable for one reason or another to study under the guidance of a sculptor will find in this book a basic plan for beginning and advice and suggestions for continuing their study. They should remember, however, that sculpture involves craftsmanship as well as creative expression. The hobbyist and the dilettante will do better to choose a field requiring less strenuous mental and physical effort, and one with fewer disciplines.

There are easy methods of producing three-dimensional objects which might broadly be called sculpture. But for the beginner, short cuts are false economy of time and effort; what is produced is of small importance compared to what is learned, and learning always involves general principles rather than specific solutions.

The average layman may find a better understanding of sculpture through reading this book. Some feeling for materials and understanding of the sculptor's thought processes, even though of an indirect nature, will help in the development of sculptural appreciation. This kind of reader should also look only for a basis of understanding and not for a final answer. Real appreciation depends not on what the observer knows but on what he feels and understands.

While most of the book is devoted to materials and techniques which are explained in sufficient detail to be of immediate use, they are presented as part of the creative process and not as ends in themselves. They are discussed in terms of general principles of sculpture, with direction toward a deeper understanding which can be applied beyond the specific problem and which is not restricted by the limited data of a formula.

Many tools and materials used in sculpture, especially those recently developed, are not widely distributed. A list of the tools and materials discussed in this book, along with a partial list of manufacturers, is contained in Appendix 2.

The illustrations in the book are of work by the author and his students at the Newcomb School of Art of Tulane University. They were selected to illustrate certain principles contained in the text rather than to present individual works of art. Descriptive titles were omitted because I believe that the techniques should not be isolated or studied apart from the text. To do so would be to miss one of the most important contentions of the book. If the text is studied and understood, the illustrations will be clear enough for reference without titles.

Finally, a few words about terminology. There are two terms occurring frequently throughout the book that require some attention here. A general understanding of the words *form* and *creative* is essential to even the most elementary discussion of sculpture. *Form*, especially, has a number of meanings which often cause confusion. Its use as a noun in this book is usually restricted to one definition: *the visual objective realization of a mental concept.* Form may be either two-dimensional or three-dimensional. In either case, *formless* refers to a lack of expressive organization, not to a lack of the depth dimension. At times, the use is closely related to that of *design,* but it includes more. *The form is the sum total of all that is perceived in a design.* Form is always used in the singular when referring to one object, being the frame of reference for the perception of any given mass. The human body, for instance, is a form composed of related shapes, not smaller forms.

The head, considered apart from the body, becomes the form containing the features which are subordinate masses. Similarly, a group of figures is a form, and the individual figures are shapes within it. A group of sculptures may be referred to as a group of forms, since the organization of each is independent of the others. When the word is used in any variation from this definition, the special meaning is made clear.

In its general sense, *to create* means simply to bring into existence. But one may create sculpture that does not have the quality of creativeness. As the term is used in this book, it means not just making something, although the creator is often not conscious of more than that. In our terms, creativeness springs from a deep-seated need for self-expression through communication, and presupposes that one has something important to express. Newness and originality are implicit in a creation in varying amounts, but being different for the sake of being different is not being creative. Also we cannot, without stretching the definition, say that children making mud pies are being creative. They are expressing little more than their need for self-expression. However, as their concepts develop—as they have more to say—this same urge toward self-expression becomes the basis for truly creative work.

We can speak meaningfully of the creative aspects of sculpture only in broad terms and in reference to specific objects. For instance, we may say that there is the nucleus of creativeness in the mud pies of children and that the "mud pie" shown in Figure 12 (page 35) is a more advanced creative concept derived from something seen in a seahorse. Development of the creative capacity may be further illustrated by comparing this student work with some of Rodin's bronze sculptures which, regardless of one's opinion of them as sculpture, exemplify tremendous creative energy. From this and other similar comparisons we can surmise that everyone has some creative urge, that the development of this creativeness is closely tied in with the intellectual and emotional growth of a person, and that the creative capacity varies among individuals.

In the first few chapters, the evolving creative factor can be traced through the sequence of the illustrations, though this is not the organizational plan of the whole book.

1· The Nature of Sculpture

SCULPTURE is man's expression to man through three-dimensional form. In the widest sense, nearly all man-made forms contain sculptural problems. Much of the designing of three-dimensional objects, from fountain pens to skyscrapers, is determined by "what looks best" —that is, by visual expressiveness. Given a problem of designing a desk lamp, one can achieve a number of equally valid solutions of functional lighting; but of the possible solutions, some will look better than others. The difference here is a sculptural matter. In the designing of objects, all problems of form not controlled by mechanistic function are determined sculpturally. This is not meant to imply that function and visual expression are incompatible. On the contrary, form should express function; but it may and usually does express more.

The expressive forms we create are a bridge between our environment and our personal outlook. The form must be shaped so that it

1

fits into our idea world. As ideas change, new forms that reflect these new concepts are created. Specifically, the field of sculpture is concerned with the expression of ideas in three-dimensional form, apart from any utilitarian function. It is here that the creator of three-dimensional objects finds the greatest opportunities for creativeness and expressiveness. This book deals with sculpture in that restricted sense.

Need for Sculpture

The need for expressive form seems to have existed since the beginning of man's history, if we can judge from the stream of sculpture that has come down to us. Considering the number of objects now being bought primarily for their visual appeal, we realize that this need has not diminished. True, it is hard to consider as sculpture the objects on the average whatnot shelf, but they point to people's need for sculptural form.

Perhaps our desire for quantity has hampered the fulfillment of our sculptural needs. These whatnot sculptures are designed to be sold cheaply. The manufacturers capitalize on the fact that most people will give up quality for a saving in price. Looking about the average gift shop, one is appalled not only at the bad taste shown in the objects but also by the quantity that is sold. In sculpture, man has always striven to express the highest cultural manifestation of his time; but these gift-shop objects are designed to appeal to the lowest taste level. So it may be wrong to consider them sculpture, even though we must admit that they serve, to some extent, the same purpose served by sculpture.

Modern Sculpture

Modern sculpture—that is, sculpture created in our times and expressive of it—has become separated from the lives of average people. Except for a few pieces on public buildings and in museums and private collections, sculpture remains in the sculptor's studio. Though most sculptors are quite willing to sell their work when approached by an appreciative buyer, it is not created primarily for that purpose. Nearly all modern sculpture results from an inner urge of the sculptors to seek self-expression rather than from public demand. There is always hope of an understanding audience, but the sculptor finds few that can understand his language. His need for communication, however, drives him on to set up his own standards and to continue creating in spite of his realization that he is crying in the wilderness. Ideally, there should be an equilibrium between the sculptor and a public which demands the best of the sculptor's ability; in this way the needs of both could be met.

Tradition

Part of the lack of understanding and appreciation the layman has of today's sculpture is due to a misunderstanding of the term *tradition*. We are so accustomed to hearing "modern" posed against "tradition" that most of us assume that the two are at opposite poles. Actually sculptural tradition has made a more or less unbroken path right up to modern sculpture and including it. The tradition has been broken only when held back and allowed to stagnate. Sculptors in the great periods have always created forms expressive of their particular civilizations, making use of all available materials and techniques. New resources and philosophies of life should result in new forms. These forms, as we have said, should be a kind of bridge between the physical and spiritual lives of the people. Contemporary sculpture, rather than a break in the great tradition, is a break with a lag in this tradition which reached one of its lowest levels in the nineteenth century. In the Western world sculpture had been degenerating since the Renaissance and had drifted so far from sculptural tradition that a seemingly violent revolution was necessary to swing it back in the right direction.

In the twentieth century much progress has been made toward recovering tradition, but until modern sculpture is reintegrated into contemporary life and generally understood by the public, we cannot consider tradition to be re-established. Eventually, it will be accepted as a normal expression of our times, just as modern industrial design (which is only a step or two removed from sculpture) is accepted. In the meantime, various efforts are being made to enlighten the public on sculpture, particularly in college art departments and in certain museums.

How to Look at Sculpture

Sculptural expression is a direct visual experience, something which cannot be explained with words. Verbally, the most anyone can do is to clear a path for the vision, clear away the overgrowth of false ideas, to help the real message enter through the eyes. Words are cumbersome when applied to sculpture, and we find it necessary to analyze, rationalize, and generalize, where such is nearly impossible, in order to make any verbal sense at all. However, the gap between the tastes of the average person and the standards of contemporary sculpture is so great that words are our only recourse in establishing a basic understanding. Looking at sculpture is the only way to appreciate it, but you must know how to look at it.

Perhaps never before in history has it been necessary to tell people how to look at art. This phenomenon has grown out of a separation of art from other human activities during the last few centuries. Regardless of how and why this situation developed, we seem to be faced with the problem of "explaining" art to the public. The difficulty of this task is increased by our proximity to the cultural lag of the late nineteenth century. Most people readily, almost proudly, admit they know nothing about art, but faced with a piece of modern sculpture they make statements that prove they are actually full of prejudices. These prejudices are based on a misconception of sculptural values.

The person who asks: "What does this represent?" is on the wrong track. Sculpture does not represent; it *is*. While sculptors usually find in nature their inspiration for creating forms (as we shall see later), what they create is an entity in itself. Looking at sculpture, then, we must remember that we are looking at a *new thing,* not a copy of something. We should forget prejudices as far as possible or try to push them out of the way. Comparison to a preconceived ideal or to other sculpture may be made later, but for a while let the sculpture speak in its own terms. We must not anticipate what the sculpture is to say, nor should we expect to be able to verbalize its message.

4

Our first reactions may not be pleasant; new things are not easily accepted, and usually the newer they are, the less pleasant they will be. We should not be too hasty in judging. That which is easily accepted may soon become meaningless and boring; unpleasant reactions in the beginning may develop into significant meanings later. It is sometimes startling to realize that many things which we accept were rejected at the time of their creation. This is true of Wagner's music which often during his lifetime was ruled out as too barbaric by many, including some reputable music critics.

So far, we have emphasized the passive approach in looking at sculpture, but if we are to get the most out of a sculpture we must do more than let it affect us. Once we are on speaking terms with the piece, we must enter into the creative process. Just as the sculptor is inspired by the creative unity of the universe, so we can draw inspiration from his work to satisfy our own creative needs. We become re-creators, and in this process we receive not only the vicarious pleasure of re-creating the particular thing before us, but we become more aware of our universe and our own problems of expression. It is on this level of reciprocal communication that sculpture fulfills its function most completely.

Of course one cannot learn to appreciate sculpture in a few easy lessons. It will take time, experience, and effort. The prejudices mentioned above are not so easily dismissed. And as they are discarded, we must replace them with new ideals. These, too, will give way to still newer ones as we grow artistically.

The relationship of the rational to the intuitive in art appreciation is hard to determine, and it is not our purpose here to do more than to touch on it. Certainly this relationship varies among individuals and within individuals at various times. In most cases it would seem that the greatest understanding and appreciation come through the intuition. Rationally, we are too apt to become literal and to verbalize to the extent of missing much of the visual expression. But the only way we can strengthen our intuition is through a great deal of direct experience, and in the beginning it is helpful to have a rational set of values to lean on as we work toward a more complete intuitive understanding.

2· The Elements of Sculpture

AS WE STUDY contemporary sculpture, we find that it is not so very different from sculpture of any other period. There are common denominators in all good sculpture that change only in degree of emphasis. By studying these basic principles, we can establish a set of values for judging sculpture.

All good sculpture is a fusion of three elements: *idea* (subject matter), *form* (three-dimensional design), and *technical means* (materials and techniques). These elements are so interrelated, the one dependent upon the other, that their true values exist only when the three are seen as a unit. In other words, the whole is greater than the sum total of the parts. In taking a thing apart to find out what makes it "tick," we destroy the relationships that cause the "tick." Hence we will not try to isolate these elements completely but we will discuss them as a unit with the emphasis placed on one at a time.

6

Sculptural Ideas

First, we find that all great sculptures result from concepts that have an *affinity for expression in the third dimension*. We will call these concepts *sculptural ideas*. Sculptural ideas must be visually expressive, the meaning implicit in the form itself. If they need explaining or lean heavily on titles, they are weak. While the "story behind the sculpture" may be interesting and may give overtones of meaning to the form, the sculptural value is purely visual. The Statue of Liberty is a bad sculptural idea because it is not visually expressive. One has to be told what it symbolizes before any meaning can be attached to it. On the other hand, most Gothic sculptures are good sculptural ideas because they "speak visually." We do not have to know what they symbolize to find their meaning. Through their forms they tell us things which words could never express.

In relation to space, sculptural ideas are ideas of actuality—that is, they are concepts of objects that will exist tactually as well as visually in space. Thus, they become involved with materials such as stone, wood, or metal, and must conform with the physical laws governing these substances. For instance, an idea for a stone carving must be controlled by the characteristics of stone, regardless of any other content. Form, concept, and material can never be completely separated. We find it impossible to conceive of a three-dimensional shape without having at least a vague vision of actual physical materials, or conversely, when we think of materials we have in mind some mass-shape. We can, however, give our major consideration to either of these inseparables. Our material may be only so much suitable substance to hold our shape-idea, or the form concept only an excuse for working with the material, but form and material in both cases must be integrated in order to be sculpturally valid.

Sculptural ideas are abstracted from time—that is, a sculptural idea is the essence of a time sequence, not the sequence itself or any single part of it. The incidental and accidental should be eliminated and the timeless aspects emphasized. For example, a person walking goes through many movements, but, looked at separately, no one gesture adequately expresses the idea of walking. An abstract movement—

7

that is, one distilled from all the others—must be made in order to establish the idea of walking motion in a static form. Egyptian carvings are good examples of this timelessness in sculpture. Perhaps the opposite of this kind of sculpture is best illustrated by some of the late-nineteenth-century pieces with their lavish detail and accidental and incidental form such as that found in "La Marseillaise" by François Rude or in the work of Carpeaux and Dalou.

Almost all sculptural ideas are abstractions of organic life; inorganic form such as clothes and props usually have been subordinated to the living form. The sculptor has had as one of his aims, possibly his principal aim, the freeing of these time-bound organic forms, abstracting them in a permanent material. Wisely, he has, in most cases, realized that literal copying of shapes would not achieve his purpose. To reproduce the momentary form in another material would have resulted not only in a transgression on the material, but in a dead copy; what he wanted was a thing with life that would continue to live as long as there was someone to see it.

Sculptural ideas are infinite; they may be inspired by rationalization, direct response to nature, such indirect stimuli as the dance, music, literature, or, more usually, by combinations of two or more of these. The form which the sculptor visualizes springs forth simultaneously with the idea; in other words, the sculptor "thinks" in three-dimensional form. Usually this form concept is vague to begin with and has to be worked out in the later stages of development of the sculpture.

Three-dimensional Design

A good design results from, or along with, a good idea; and the design is good only in terms of its materials. Ideally, the entire synthesis of these elements takes place in the mind, before the actual object is started. This rarely happens, however, and it is just as well, since, if it did, the sculptor would miss much of the pleasure and excitement of seeing his creation unfold. What usually happens is this: one has a more or less vague and flexible synthesis in mind when beginning, and as the sculpture progresses it becomes clearer and more positive. It is in this working phase that a knowledge or feeling for three-dimensional design is most helpful. There are many decisions to make, and one must have a basis for deciding on them.

Three-dimensional design is the construction of *expressive order in space*. To help understand its importance and place in sculptural problems, let us consider for a moment the "seeing process." Our eyes are not as efficient as most people think. We see two-dimensionally, except for the small amount of binocular vision which results from our eyes being set apart, so that each presents a slightly different picture to the brain. The third dimension is known in the mind partly through binocular vision, partly through composites of two-dimensional views gathered as we move about an object, but mostly through our sense of touch and our own existence and movement in space. We have a feeling for depth and a knowledge of it, but we do not literally *see* it. Then, too, we see only in terms of light reflected from planes. We can see surfaces, but not the underlying structure nor the significant inner life. This is learned from experience and intuition. Thus, we find that there is much discrepancy between what we see and what we know.

A three-dimensional design presupposes an idea from which a system of order can be derived. This order is made visually expressive, enabling us to show to some extent what is known. Order within a design creates a greater awareness of existence. A sculptor sometimes has a preference for a particular natural form and will make a number of studies of it. Consciously or unconsciously, he finds in it an inner significance of universal order, which he tries to express through various modifications in his designs.

For the sake of clarity, then, we will say that the purpose of three-dimensional design is twofold, but we will find upon closer study that both ends are fulfilled simultaneously. First, we are faced with the problem of presenting to the mind a three-dimensional form through a series of relatively two-dimensional views; and second, we want to express certain feelings or truths through the arrangements of the parts of the form. In the process of designing, we must relate the views so that they are easily linked together in the mind, making one mental image rather than isolated aspects of several things. Each view must fit into the order of the whole and be a vital part of it. At the same time and in conjunction with this problem, the unity of expression is fulfilled; a form cannot be seen as one thing if it expresses something different from various views. For instance, in a sculpture of a woman weeping, the entire form must be expressive of grief whether seen from the front, side, or back. If not, the sculpture will present conflicting stimuli to the brain and the result will be a weak, meaningless mental image. In other words, good three-dimensional design presents an object to the mind which speaks of the same thing from all views.

Certain means are used to create expressive design. To begin with, the substance of which the design is made exists relatively in space. Just as sound and silence exist only in relation, space and substance activate each other. In music varying degrees of emphasis are placed on sound and silence; in sculpture both substance and space contribute to the expression in varying degrees. The design may be primarily space-displacing, as most stone carving, or space-enclosing, as some metal sculptures. Each design is seen through, and in relation to, its "atmosphere," the activated space in and around the form. Then, the manner in which space is activated gives us the basis for a particular expression. We "feel" the weight of space-displacing mass; or we "feel" the control, the "taming" and realness of a volume of enclosed space. In the former, we establish mass with planes, both flat and convex, pushing out into space; in the latter, our means are basically lines and concave planes, drawing around and pulling space inward.

Planes

Geometrically, a plane is defined as a surface such that, if any two of its points are connected by a straight line, that line always lies wholly on the surface; or every point in that line is on the surface. However, for our purposes, we need not be so exacting. Sculpturally, planes are areas of surface defined by a more or less abrupt change in direction, and may be either flat or curved—that is, two-dimensional or three-dimensional. The planes of a cube are six flat areas of equal size defined by right-angle turns; a sphere has only one continuous convex area which constitutes its one plane. Often a thin mass, such as a sheet of metal or a board is referred to as a plane when the proportions are such that the thickness is negligible. In most organic form changes in direction are so subtle and varied that in our process of seeing we tend to organize toward simpler geometric shapes. We think of apples as being spherical and mountains as conical or pyramidal. By geometricizing form we present a sharper spatial statement because directions, and therefore dimensions, are clearer.

When a mass in a three-dimensional design is composed of many subtle changes in direction, these planes are often organized so that a simple, over-all form "envelope" results. In many carvings, for instance, one can still see the shape of the original block. This "envelope" is composed of what we will call *virtual planes*—that is, planes partially defined and partially imagined. These virtual planes are important, both in studying natural form and in constructing designs. With them we establish three-dimensional references within which we can get at more subtle qualities.

Lines

Lines do not exist in the third dimension. The phenomena that we see as lines are of three kinds: (1) outlines or the extremities of silhouettes, which are the two-dimensional extensions of planes in space from a fixed point of view, (2) junctions of planes, and (3) the axes of three-dimensional shapes in which the length is much greater than the width and depth. Very thin shapes of the latter kind, such as wire and rods, are usually seen and therefore referred to as lines. *Virtual lines*— that is, lines which seem to exist between two or more points that are closely related—are as important in the clarification of our perception as virtual planes. We often use them as a frame of reference in establishing mental pictures.

Textures

Textures are the surface qualities of substances. We develop our knowledge of them through a synthesis of tactile and visual stimulation. We learn what visual characteristics mean hardness, softness, stickiness, etc.; and we sense how the texture would feel if we touched it. Our eyes become quite keenly trained with experience so that we recognize most substances immediately from visual qualities; but very often we find ourselves touching the surface to get a fuller perception of texture.

Sculpturally, we are interested in several aspects of texture: (1) texture as it expresses the structural characteristics of our materials, such as wood grain, metal sheen, etc.; (2) texture as it expresses our control over the shaping of the material, such as modeled surfaces in clay, tool marks on stone or wood; (3) translated textures—that is, textures inspired by our subject matter and interpreted in our material; and, finally, (4) the light-reflecting capacities of textures, such as the emphasizing of projections by polishing and the enlivening of recessed areas by breaking up the surface into small highlights and shadows.

Color

The chiaroscuro, or pattern of light and dark in a sculpture, is sometimes referred to as color. This, however, is a matter of plane organization; our use of the word here is in its more usual sense of hue.

As a plastic element, color plays a much smaller part in sculpture than it does in painting. In the third dimension we do not have the degree of control over light that one finds in a two-dimensional design. Unless the form has a constant light source and is viewed from a fixed position, the color relationships continually change. Local colors—that is, the actual colors of materials—are modified by the quality, quantity, and position of the light source. For this reason, most sculpture is done in a uniform local color. This simplifies the problem of unifying tonal relationships of light and shadow. Polychromatic form, even on a limited scale, greatly complicates the designing process. One must be constantly aware of the numerous ways color and shape affect each other under varying light conditions and shifting points of view. This problem is discussed further in Chapter 4.

Masses and Volumes

For our purposes, masses or solids are three-dimensional, space-displacing shapes defined by planes; volumes are virtual negative masses, or three-dimensional areas of space partially enclosed by planes or lines. In our terms then, a mountain is a mass and a valley is a volume. We also consider a group of closely related solid shapes, such as the fingers in a clenched fist, a mass. A design is said to be massive when its form is predominately solid shapes organized into a simple over-all mass. In a volume, definiteness in the shape of the space depends on the degree of enclosure, but since we are concerned only with the visual aspects, much of the definition of the area must depend on virtual planes. For example, looking at a hollow hemisphere, we see a volume defined by a curved actual plane and a flat virtual plane. If the shape is changed so that it becomes more of a complete sphere, the size of the virtual plane diminishes and the visual effectiveness of the volume is decreased proportionately. However, a complete spherical volume can be described by lines created with wire or rods provided they are spaced so that the enclosed space can be seen through the virtual planes between the lines.

Unity and Variety

With the elements of planes, lines, textures, and color we can set about organizing masses and volumes into a design. First let us see what the controlling factors are in organizing in the third dimension. All good designs are unified—that is, each part is an essential contribution to the whole, and this whole determines the character of each part. To explain further what we mean by unity, let us use as examples two geometric shapes, the sphere and the cylinder. The sphere is the simpler, since its surface is one consistently curved plane. A sphere could be reconstructed accurately from a small area of its surface. The cylinder is much more complex because it involves a variable relationship between two independent dimensions. In other words, all spheres are identical except for size, but there are different *kinds* of cylinders. We can say then that whereas the sphere automatically has a mathematical oneness, we have to establish this quality in a cylinder, and, in a very limited sense, some expression of unity enters into its construction. If the difference between the height and width is great, as in a piece of wire, the visual identity of the cylinder is lost because of a lack of unity in proportion. On the other hand, if the height and width are equal, the cylinder concept is clearer but the shape is uninteresting. In both cases there is a tendency for the mind not to respond to the shapes. In the first case, most people will see not a cylinder but a line, and in the second, the proportion is simply too monotonous to hold our attention. Sculpturally, then, unity should be a balance between visual clarity and interest.

To simplify problems in discussions, however, we will refer to these two aspects of unity at times as "unity" in the sense of oneness and "variety" as meaning variations in relationships. In these terms we can say that as organic form approaches the geometric, it becomes more easily comprehended in space and more unified; and as geometric form approaches the organic, it becomes more varied and gains in interest and meaning. Our form problem, then, is one of balance between unity and variety.

Principles of Order

We create unity and variety in a design through various principles of order. Before we go into these, it might be wise to advise the reader that these principles are suggested aids for beginners, and not criteria for designs. We must judge designs as total visual expressions; if the whole is bad then none of the parts is right. These principles of order may help us in finding the right visual solution, but they are not ends in themselves and following them will not guarantee good results. We must also remember that the whole is more important than the parts, and that the application of these principles is controlled by the total concept.

Balance

We are concerned with two aspects of balance in sculpture: the relationship of mass to support (law of gravitation), and the distribution of interest or the balance of attraction (attention-value of our four elements: planes, lines, texture, and color). In both cases our own sense of physical balance is involved. We "feel" the effect of the arrangement of masses and support as we feel the effect of gravity on our own

14

bodies in various positions. Balance of attraction is closely related to two other principles discussed later: contrast and movement. Some parts of a form attract more attention than others through contrast of parts or through a pattern of movements. The method of balancing this interest is one of the expressive means of design.

The possibilities of arrangement are of two kinds: formal or bisymmetrical balance and occult balance. In formal balance, the masses, volumes, and interest are equally distributed around vertical or horizontal axes. Geometrical forms, for instance, are bisymmetrically balanced. The effect of this kind of arrangement is usually cold, static, and dignified; unity is easily attained, but it is apt to be monotonous. Occult balance is achieved by organizing the parts so that a dynamic equilibrium results. It is a more interesting and expressive way of arranging shapes. A large mass may be balanced with smaller masses, and solids balanced with space. Parts may be off balance, provided that they contribute to the over-all balance of the total design.

The only rule for balance is to judge by eye and try to feel for the right arrangement. We can say, however, that usually formally balanced designs tend toward expressions of repose or contained tension, while occultly balanced designs are more dynamic and expressive of agitation or explosive vitality.

Proportion

Proportion pertains to size relationships: (1) of the total form, height to width to depth; and (2) within the design, relative sizes of the parts to the whole. Each design determines its own laws of proportion; and the reference point is the sculptural concept, not nature itself. While nature is our greatest teacher of proportion, we must remember that once we isolate a part of nature, tear it from its context, so to speak, and transfer it to another material, we must make certain compensations. In other words, natural proportions usually give us a starting point for a system of size relationships which we work out in developing our sculptural concept.

There are various rules of mechanical measurement, such as the system of dynamic symmetry used by the Greeks, which assure good proportions. However, mechanical methods have a very limited—that is, a

15

two-dimensional—value in sculpture, since there is constant distortion in the depth dimension. It is helpful to know that equal divisions and 1:2 ratios are usually monotonous, and 3:5 ratios are more interesting. But the final judgment of proportion must be based on a question: "Does the proportion express what I have to say?"

Exaggeration in proportion, through expansion and contraction, is part of the expressive language of form. In the development of our visual symbols, size relationships are an important factor. We tend to exaggerate what is significant to us and sometimes to eliminate less meaningful elements altogether. In our designing, then, we may make use of proportion to attain emphasis.

Material demands must be met with certain shape proportions. A leaf carved in stone cannot have the same proportions as a natural leaf. If we study our materials in their raw states, as they exist normally in nature, we can find many clues to the kinds of proportions they demand. Then the study of organic form will offer us shapes which, exaggerated to greater or less degree, will fit these proportions. Or we may start from another point: the organic shape idea may come first and the proper material, the material which can truthfully contain these proportions, is then selected.

Movement

We may define movement in sculpture as the visual stimulation in a static form which produces a sensation similar to actual movement in space. This may be achieved in a number of ways: (1) along the axes of elongated forms, (2) along a progression of planes, (3) along a series of points or areas of contrast, (4) along the path of lines, and (5) by representational associations. Movement in a design serves a double-edged visual function. It activates space in such a way that we "see" what the eyes do not see—that is, we are made aware of a life force that is not actually there, and it creates a greater awareness of existence in space by enabling our eyes to see more of the third dimension than we ordinarily see. It links together the two-dimensional pictures our eyes send to the brain. Many of the expressive characteristics in a design are established by the qualities of its dominant movements. Straight vertical movements produce effects of strength; horizontal movements, of repose; and flowing movements, of grace. Nature, again, is our guide to expressive movements. The actual movements of an animal can be seen abstractly in his form even when he is still; the smooth gracefulness of a deer's movements and the lumbering steps of the elephant can be seen in every part of their respective bodies. This unity of form expression is easily seen in humans; when we are dejected we fall into a pose of descending movements; when agitated, into zig-zag movements; and so on. Seen in a piece of sculpture, these movements recall corresponding feelings in our own bodies. We react empathically to them.

Repetition

Similarity might be a better term for our purposes here, since we do not necessarily mean exactness in using the word *repetition*. The strongest unifying factor in a design is the likeness of parts to the whole. In plant and animal life we find repetition of shape characteristics; the leaf is similar to the tree, and animal shapes have the character of the whole animal.

Walking around a sculpture, we build up the total image in our minds. If shapes, movements, and textures are recalled, the various views will seem to belong together and will form a more integrated and meaningful image. In some cases, to obtain rhythm or emphasis, we may want to use rather exact repetition, but we must avoid monotony. Parts may be identical in shape but different in size; movements may vary only slightly from each other; the same patterns of texture may be repeated in areas of various sizes and shapes. Balance, proportion, and visual judgment must be our guides in repetition of this kind.

Contrast

To some extent we can say that contrast is the opposite of repetition, and yet often it serves the same function. For instance, emphasis may be achieved through either repeating or contrasting. The two also work hand in hand in creating variety within unity; a solid shape may be recalled in an open shape, and two masses may be repeated in shape but contrasted in size. Contrast is the inflective quality in our sculptural language. As we increase it we raise the volume, so to speak, and as we decrease it, we create subtlety. From our original idea we establish an over-all tone which is to be carried out in the design—that is, we decide whether it will be loud or soft in key. Then, within this tone, contrast becomes a relative matter. In a subtle form, sufficient contrast should be used for emphasis but not to the extent that unity is destroyed. In a more bombastic kind of design, subtleties would be lost, and the unity can be maintained only by charging each part with enough contrast for it to hold its own.

Unity of the Principles of Order

As we have seen, these principles of order cannot be treated as isolated rules. Besides controlling the elements of planes, lines, colors, and textures, they must be thoroughly interlaced. We establish balance of movement, contrast of movement, repetition or contrast of proportion, etc. We have also found that these principles are implicit in nature; we might say that as all man-made objects contain sculptural problems, all natural forms contain solutions to these problems.

Summarizing three-dimensional design, we can thus say:

With	*planes*	we create	*unity*	of	*masses*	through	*balance*
	lines		*variety*		*volumes*		*proportion*
	texture						*movement*
	color						*repetition*
							contrast

Materials and Techniques

Since the major part of this book is devoted to materials and techniques, they will be introduced only generally here. As one of the elements in our sculptural trinity of idea, form, and technical means, we must consider materials and techniques creatively. The close relationship between form and material has been mentioned earlier, but technique, too, plays an important part in the creative process. The structural characteristics of material determine various techniques for shaping it: basically these are carving, modeling, and constructing, each presenting possibilities and limitations within a given material. Thus, in the relationship between form and technical means, material is the general control and technique is the special control. For instance, one can do things with wood construction that would be unthinkable in wood carving, but the nature of the material sets limits over forms created with either technique.

Techniques in sculpture can be easily misunderstood. On the one hand, they may be treated as the proverbial stepchild, something to avoid wherever possible and to contend with grudgingly. This attitude grows out of a misconception of freedom in creating. The person who avoids learning techniques ends up in frustration and confusion; not only does lack of techniques prevent him from controlling material, but technique is implicit in the sculptural concept. We conceive within a general technical knowledge which is expanded with every creative manifestation. A twenty-story building was conceivable only when building techniques made it possible. When this was achieved, taller buildings were conceivable, and so on. Just as in the creation of form we must think in terms of a given material, in the total conception of these forms we are limited by our knowledge of how to shape this material. Unconsciously, perhaps, our technique begins at the very inception of an idea.

Getting back to the misconception of freedom, we see that where there is little technical understanding there is little freedom of creation, mentally as well as physically. True freedom can be attained only through discipline. Rather than running from techniques, we must learn them so well that we think through them, not around them. This kind of knowledge results from a continual revitalization of the creative process: it cannot be learned in a vacuum. Here we can begin to see the other extreme of technical misunderstanding. When technique becomes an end in itself—a sheer demonstration of skill in handling tools and materials—it is no longer subservient to its purpose, and creativeness is smothered. Along with mastering techniques, we have to learn how they can be synthesized in the process of creating. This can be learned only through direct experience.

Generally, there are several ways of handling every material: wood can be carved or constructed; metal, constructed or cast; stone, cast or carved, etc. Each method can exploit different characteristics of the material. A technique is either good or bad for our purpose in so far as it facilitates the unity of idea, form, and material. The quickest method of shaping is not necessarily the best, and is very often detrimental to the unity of expression. The criterion must be synthesis, not speed, and this becomes a kind of growing process that involves time and change. Good techniques allow for modifications within the over-all restriction of the original concept, so that as work in the material progresses, sensitive changes can be made. Some techniques allow a greater margin for changes than others. Later, in the discussion of wood-carving processes, two methods will be presented. One involves cutting off large masses of wood with a band saw; the other is a process of gradually releasing the form by taking off small amounts at a time. In the first, a relatively clear concept of the final form must be established before cutting, as there are few chances for change; in the other system, the form may seek its own actualization to a large extent. Further comparison of the two techniques as teaching methods are made later.

Summary

Throughout this chapter, the unity of the sculptural trinity—idea, form, and technical means—has been emphasized. The fact that we have been unable to talk about one without bringing in the others clearly demonstrates their inseparability. The three are interdependent and must be judged as a unit; one cannot be considered more vital to the sculptural expression than the others.

Another conclusion which will throw additional light on the nature of sculpture can be drawn from what has been said: our process of perception is also a synthesis of three elements—the intellectual, emotional, and physical (sensory). The relationship of this trinity to idea, form, and technical means is obvious. The subject matter primarily evokes intellectual response; the design, emotional reactions; and the handling of materials, sensory stimulation. But remember, our perception is a synthesis! Neither in creating nor appreciating do we make a conscious separation of these elements. A sculptor, then, through his sculpture, works directly with the three parts of perception to express himself. By emphasizing one or another of the sculptural elements, he controls his expression; but, of course, this expression is itself controlled by his own powers of perception.

3· The Problem
of Beginning

BEFORE actually getting down to work, we may profit by a few words on the student-teacher relationship. Sculpture is a creative process, and every student has a creative potential. The teacher cannot tell a student exactly how to make a piece of sculpture. The most he can do is to help the student work out his own ideas in sculptural form; to remove obstacles, especially technical ones; to establish contact with the creative potential and encourage it to grow. This requires the active, not passive, cooperation of the student. If he waits for the teacher to dictate every move, if he does only what he is told to do, there is no chance for the teacher to make contact with his creative abilities. The aim of good teaching is to give the student a firm foundation on which to develop his self-hood; teaching should begin thought, not end it. Creativeness is based on independence, and we should start developing this at the beginning.

1

2

Another important element in the teaching-learning process is the attitude of the student toward his work. The value of student problems is purely educational; to think of the object as an end in itself is wrong. His work is good only in so far as it indicates that he has learned something about sculpture. The piece that is made for the mantle of a favorite aunt is doomed, educationally, from the beginning. What the student should take with him at the end of a course of study in sculpture is not a group of finished works, but the knowledge, understanding, and desire to continue creating, and at least the rudiments of self-development.

The only way sculpture can be learned is by doing. Theories and dissertations may clarify our thinking and prepare the ground, but without application to direct experience, they are meaningless. The big difficulty in doing always lies in beginning properly; and in sculpture the problem is increased because we cannot separate the parts of sculpture and study them individually. We found that idea, form, and technical means were so entwined that getting at one involves the others. The best solution of the problem, then, is to do a series of studies on a level simple enough so that it will be possible to consider all three together, although one element is emphasized at a time.

Unity to Variety

We will begin with the simplest idea content—geometric form—and the easiest material to handle—clay—and study the form problem of variety within unity. First, we will make a rough sketch between one and two inches high in the following manner: select a basic geometric form —sphere, cube, cylinder, or cone—and construct it approximately in clay. Studying it, we find there is much unity but little variety; we get bored with looking at it in a short time. Now with a knife cut into the planes, removing portions of the mass to break this monotony. This requires some planning and a system. If our basic form is a sphere, we may cut flat planes for contrast, or repeat the spherical idea in smaller planes. If we use a pyramid or a cube, contrasting planes and proportion can be used for variety. (See the sketches in Figures 1 and 2.) Notice how each change activates space in a different manner. The

3

4

5

6

designing is done entirely within the original geometric form, and a sufficient amount of its surface is retained so that unity is not lost. These sketches can be done quickly, and a number of them should be made for the purpose of studying various principles of order. Some will have more sculptural interest—that is, variety within unity—than others. Look carefully at the ones you prefer, to see if you can tell why they are better. Then, select the one that appears to be best. Three-dimensionality—movement, balance, proportion—should be considered in making the choice.

Clay and the Modeling Technique

We now have a sketch of a sculptural concept. The next step is to develop it into final form. Our material is clay, our technique will be modeling, and we must pause long enough to give each some consideration. Clay will be discussed in detail in Chapter 8 when we discuss terra cotta, so here we will cover only the aspects that pertain to the immediate problem and the technique we will be using. Modeling clay is a mixture of earth substances and sufficient water to give it a consistency of bread dough. In the raw state, it is plastic—that is, capable of being pushed or built into almost any shape. When it is fired (baked), it attains a hardness similar to a brick. You will learn a great many of its characteristics in working with it.

The technique of modeling is a process of building around a pre-conceived axis and within previsualized boundaries. In other words, you must have a reasonably clear idea of the form before the building starts. The sketch (Figure 3) will help considerably in this visualizing. You start by establishing the height, building a rough core 6 or 8 inches high around this axis using relatively small pieces of clay (Figure 4). Turning the work continually so as to build *three-dimensionally,* you establish the major planes of the design. One very important rule to keep in mind is always to *underbuild.* That is to say, in clay modeling you should build up to the final form gradually without overbuilding and having to cut off any of the clay. Of course, mistakes and changes will be made, but you should avoid them as far as possible. When it is necessary to cut away some of the clay you have built, always take off more than is necessary and build back the proper amount. And you must check the sketch continually to see that your work is progressing properly.

Up to this point the fingers and a knife have been our tools. As you get closer to the surface smaller bits of clay are used, and it is necessary to put them on with a modeling tool (see Figure 5). The great temptation now will be to rush the completion of the form, and to concentrate too long in one area. Consciously avoid this, working evenly over the entire form.

At the beginning the pattern of progress should be something like this: work rapidly with the clay to establish the basic core of the design, stopping frequently to check on relationships such as proportion, balance, etc. If changes are to be made they should be considered carefully, made deliberately but with freedom, and reconsidered before building further. Modeling is a process of continual building. There is never a time for pushing, pulling, or rubbing the clay. In the later stage, when sharp angles and textures are involved, the building will progress slowly.

Good modeling causes the form to grow as forms in nature grow, consistently and in all dimensions. This kind of development enables us to give the form an inner life—a reaching out into space. A rubbed, slicked down surface will destroy this life. Smoothness is a relative matter; you should aim at a consistency of texture instead (Figure 6). The form should look as though it is still growing, and the surface still becoming, rather than finished. In this way the life force is increased.

When the modeling is completed a thorough self-criticism is in order. Ask yourself if the design is an improvement over the original sketch, why and how, and compare it to other problems in the class. Much can be learned by investigating the solutions of others. Realize that although this is your creation, it is not a great work of art, but only a short step in the right direction.

If the design is to be fired, it must be hollowed out when it is "leather-hard"—that is, when the clay has dried until it has the feel and consistency of leather or hard cheese. Then it can be lifted up and carved out until the walls are about ½ inch thick. When it is thoroughly dry it can be fired. The firing process is described in Chapter 8.

Variety to Unity

In the first problem we started with and retained throughout a unifying factor, the original geometric shape. This method is most often used in the carving processes where one usually begins with a block of material and designs within it. Now we will try another approach to designing, one that is more in keeping with the technique of modeling. We will start with a variety of shapes and organize them into a unified design. To avoid complications and sidetracks, we will again restrict ourselves to basic geometric form.

With two or three shapes in mind, imagine how they can be put together to form a unified but varied design. Try to invent a system based on the principles of order, and remember the spaces around the solid masses become volumes and must be organized in the total design. Work toward a simple, over-all, three-dimensional shape; if you are designing with a pyramid and a sphere, the total shape of the design, including space enclosed with the virtual planes, may be pyramidal. A cube and a cylinder may result in a design enclosed by either one. The shapes do not have to follow the exact geometric form. Parts may be cut off or grafted on and the total form may only suggest its geometrical equivalent. (See Figures 7, 8, and 9.)

So far we have not made a sketch. Remember that it is best to think out the design as far as possible before starting with clay. The extent to which a design can be carried in the mind depends on the development of the power of visualization. This ability develops through exercise. Like a muscle, the more it is used the stronger it gets. Sketching should be used only to crystallize the mental image. It may be possible to arrive at a design by manipulating clay shapes, but this "hit-or-miss" system evades the discipline of visualizing, which is of utmost importance in sculpture. When the concept has been visualized as far as you can carry it in the mind, a small clay sketch should be made and studied as in the first problem. You will probably have to make many changes from the original mental image, but each experience of this kind will enable your mind to visualize more clearly. When making corrections and changes in the design, you should visualize these, too, before making them. In a few words, learning to create sculpture is

7

8

9

largely a matter of training the "mind's eye" to see sculptural concepts more clearly.

When several sketches have been made and the best one selected, the actual building follows much the same pattern established in the first problem. You have more masses to organize; therefore, to start with, more variety and less unity. You must create unity. The sketch will give the initial proportion, balance, and movement, but as the design develops, there will be many changes. These should be made boldly—finickiness has no place in sculptural expression—but corrections should be well thought out before being made.

Summary

At the beginning of this chapter, clay was called the simplest of sculptural materials. Probably by this time you may want to question that, so we will change the statement to read: clay is the simplest material *if it is handled properly*. Being very plastic and heavy, it has a tendency to sag under its own weight. There are always great temptations to push and squeeze the clay into shape. Pushing may change one view satisfactorily, but the amount that is pushed in comes out somewhere else. The following rules from the first problem may be established, along with a few new ones:

1. Always build with relatively small pieces of clay, first determining the height of the masses and causing them to grow out into space.

2. Work three-dimensionally over the entire design, building the larger masses first.

3. Continue this building process, using progressively smaller pieces of clay until the design is complete.

4. Underbuild rather than overbuild.

5. Consider the consequences of a change or correction before making it. There are usually two or three ways of effecting a change—use judgment in deciding the best one.

6. Use modeling tools when the fingers are unsatisfactory.

7. Do not try to shape or change the form by pushing or squeezing. Use only sufficient pressure to make the pieces of clay adhere.

8. Do not work meaninglessly; the form should be touched only when

29

you are consciously and deliberately building or cutting to make corrections.

9. Do not rub the clay. Rubbing will not make a smooth surface, but will deaden the form. Work for an evenness rather than slickness.

10. Do not try to model edges to knife-like sharpness; the nature of the material does not grant that. Relative sharpness is sufficient.

These rules sound pretty strict, but clay modeling demands much discipline. When you have learned the technique of handling clay, the rules can be ignored, but before scrapping them, be sure of your mastery.

Give the design a thorough critical analysis when it is finished. Look for the bigger things first: Has progress been made compared to the first problem? Does the form have sculptural interest? Are there interesting relationships between solids and space? Is it balanced? Is it well proportioned? Has the clay been well handled? How could the design be improved?

Carving out the inside of the form to make it hollow may be a bit more complicated than in the first problem. If the wall is cut through in any place, water can be worked into the clay from the inside and the hole filled with "leather-hard" clay which has also been moistened.

With these two rather simple problems, we have experienced at least a small part of the creative process. Thus far, emphasis has been on three-dimensional design. However, the clay-modeling technique received much of our attention and idea content played its part as well. There are many things to learn yet, and the learning will be faster if we follow a system similar to the modeling technique; we should get a clear start and build bit by bit, three-dimensionally, on that which has been learned.

4· Transformation of Nature into Sculpture

NOW that we have had an introductory experience in controlling form, let us investigate some possibilities of subject matter. The world is full of it—the problem is one of selection. Before we set about looking for a suitable subject, it will be helpful to have some idea of the process of abstracting from nature.

Visual Abstraction

Much of the average person's confusion about modern art stems from a lack of understanding of visual abstraction and a misconception of what we actually *see*. No attempt will be made here to give a complete explanation of this complex subject, but we can establish a basis for greater understanding. Such understanding will come through the process of abstracting from nature.

Visual abstraction is the organizing of plastic essences into meaning-ful order. We see through visual abstractions or symbols, and usually we take time to see only enough to recognize objects or to verify expectations. Only a small part of the whole is seen, the part that is accepted as the symbol of the total. This abstraction is a simplification of the complex, but it is expressive of the whole, not just a disembodied part. These visual symbols are distilled from experience involving all our senses, but to a large extent we see only that which is familiar to us. As our experience is increased our catalogue of symbols grows; each individual's vision is not only unique to himself, but it continually changes. Most people resist these changes and try to hold on to their old symbols. Children often surprise us by pointing out things which grown-ups do not ordinarily see. This indicates that as we grow older our visual symbols become stereotyped. The creative artist differs from the average person in that he is not bound completely by the accepted symbols of his time. His vision and insight are more pene-trating. He is alert to new concepts for which there are no adequate symbols, and he is more capable of distilling new abstractions from his experience.

All art is abstract in this sense. What is called naturalism in art is simply abstraction that has become generally accepted. Corot's land-scapes were once considered very unrealistic, and certainly his system of perspective belies nature. To copy nature is utterly impossible; to attempt to do so, therefore, is pointless. The "realisticness" or "natural-ism" of art is wholly a matter of degree—not one of qualitative differ-ence between periods and styles.

Suppose we construct a human figure as imitatively as possible, using a soft, flesh-like material, glass eyes, hair, fingernails, etc.; we might also find a method of causing it to move. Even those who demand "naturalism" in art would have to admit that this is not at all what they wanted. Hence, our creative problem lies in the other direction; we must experience nature as completely as possible and then abstract from it the visual symbols that express our concepts.

Since we all have the ability to create symbols, we are all potential artists. In order to release this creative potential, we must train our-selves to be sensitive to that which is significant; we must be alert to

32

new concepts and learn to evaluate them. Creativeness grows out of the past into the future; while we must lean heavily on that which is accepted, we should also nurture our dissatisfaction with it and continually look for a more complete expression.

Abstracting Significant Form

Our problem now is to learn how we can select significant form from nature and organize it into a sculptural expression. We must start with something elementary so as to gain the maximum from the experience; if a complicated subject is chosen, other problems will overshadow the immediate task. The subject should be some simple natural form, preferably an inanimate one: leaves, fruit, seeds, bones, shells, are excellent for the purpose. Be sure to select something with an interesting character, a form to which you respond. Study it carefully, looking for stimulating shapes, textures, balance, and proportion. Try to analyze its character: are the shapes hard, soft, firm, tense, relaxed, flowing; are the lines and textures in keeping with this character? Remember that we are not copying the form but translating it into clay and human expression. A kind of design, vague at first, should begin to be visualized. Do not hurry to make a sketch; once a design is made tangible, much of the flexibility of conception is destroyed and a kind of mental fixation results which is hard to break down. The farther we can visualize before making the sketch, the better our chances of creating a synthesis between idea, form, and material.

When the idea is as clear as your powers of visualization permit, make, not one, but several sketches. Use everything you have learned about design, trying to express a feeling about the subject matter through the design elements. Keep the natural form close by and refer to it from time to time. Do not carry the sketch too far; it is only an aid for beginning the final design and should be kept small and made quickly. Rather than reworking and fussing over a sketch, make a new one; but never destroy any of them until the problem is finished. While developing the final form, you will often feel the need for more visual ideas, and some of the shape organization in these discarded sketches may prove to be helpful.

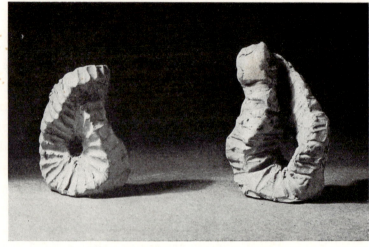

10 **11**

Figure 10 shows a seahorse which was used as the inspiration for the sketches in Figure 11. These ideas are abstract designs—that is, the characteristics of the subject are organized into meaningful order. This is the same vital process that sculptors have always followed; on a higher level, it is simply broadened in scope and intensified. Studying your sketches, you will probably find that in one you have achieved more of this than in the others. Or, perhaps, the best parts of two sketches may be combined in a third. From this sketch, begin the final design.

By now your clay modeling technique should have improved to the point where you can work freely with the material and not have to be entirely conscious of each move. Exploit this—that is, work without thinking about the technique for a few minutes at a time, and then check what you have done. If you are violating any of the rules given at the end of Chapter 3, perhaps you had better think a little more about technique as you model.

We should concentrate as far as possible on extracting the maximum

12

expression from our subject matter, but we must keep in mind that
we are expressing it through a clay design. The shapes should look
like clay and the design must "say something" about the subject. In
Figure 12 the fishlike, submarine character of the seahorse is emphasized; one feels that it belongs to the water. It is not a copy, but something new, a creation, guided in its gestation by the seahorse plus
human expression. It says something about the person who did it as
well as about the subject. The "story" it tells is more profound and
more complete than the usual superficial concept of a seahorse. A feel-

13

14

15

ing of the struggle for existence in its vast environment is abstracted from its shape and jerky movements. But this is said visually through the design and in clay's way of speaking. Another person may want to say other things about the seahorse which could be as good or better sculpture than this; but that would be a different "story"—another abstraction.

A bone was the inspiration for the expressive design shown in Figure 15. There is, perhaps, even less possibility of verbalization here than in the seahorse; but, as we have said, that is unnecessary and often detrimental in a sculpture. This form, tense and yet flowing, speaks strongly its unity and existence in space. The design does not need a title; it is an original creation, based on natural form but expressive of much more than the subject from which it was taken. In both of these sculptures (Figures 12 and 15) we see a sincere step toward abstracting nature. Our future problems will not be very different in approach; we will only go further into the process.

Wedging Grog into Clay

Now is a good time to expand our knowledge of clay techniques. Many possibilities, existing in our subject matter, were overlooked because of technical limitations. Let us further our investigation of clay and learn a new way of handling it.

As we saw, one of the disadvantages of clay is its tendency to sag under its own weight when the plasticity is right for building. This can be partially overcome by the addition of grog, which is clay that has been fired, pulverized, and screened through various meshes to limit the size of the particles. Grog may comprise up to 25 percent of the total mixture without destroying too much of the plasticity of the clay. Grades larger than 20 mesh (window screen is 18 mesh, that is, 18 openings per square inch) should not be used in small work as their coarseness hampers the modeling. The most satisfactory range for our particular problem is from 40 up to 20 mesh. The grog is mixed with the clay by a process called wedging. First, the clay is weighed and the amount of grog calculated; then the clay is laid out on the wedging table in a sheet roughly one inch thick and holes are

16

17

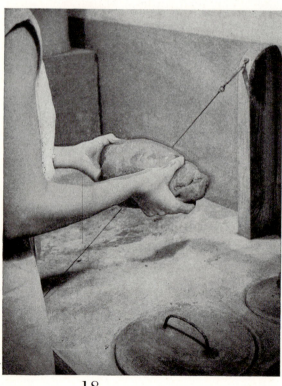

18

19

stamped in the entire surface with the thumb (Figure 16). The grog should be dampened slightly, spread over the clay, and kneaded into it with the fingers. When the grog begins to mix with the clay, the entire mass can be rolled and kneaded with the heels of the hands into a rough spherical shape. A kind of rocking motion combined with stiff-armed pushes against the table will cause the clay to slide within itself and hasten the mixing (Figure 17). As this process continues, the mass will become elongated; then it is cut in the middle by picking it up and pushing it against the taut wire stretched across the wedging table (Figure 18). Two wedge-shaped pieces will result. One is dropped on the table and the other turned over and thrown firmly against the first, so that the two wedges together form a rough rectangular block (Figure 19). The clay is kneaded and rocked until it again becomes elongated and the cutting and wedging are repeated. This process is continued until the grog is evenly distributed throughout the clay. After a little experience the action becomes rhythmical, and 15 or 20 pounds of clay can be wedged in a few minutes with little effort.

In addition to the mixing of ingredients, wedging is used to combine two consistencies of clay. If we have a quantity of clay that is too soft and sticky to use for modeling, harder clay can be mixed with it in proper amounts to arrive at the desired consistency. Wedging alone will tend to drive out some of the water from the clay, making it harder. One of the most important functions of wedging is to remove air pockets; we will be more concerned with this aspect in the section on the turning of hollow clay cylinders (pages 99-100).

The mixture of clay and grog will have a different feel from ordinary clay; there is a greater resistance in manipulation, and most beginners find it a more stimulating substance with which to work. Besides being more stable in the modeling stage, grogged clay gives off and absorbs water more readily; and this makes it possible to dampen and work over areas that have become almost leather-hard. This is discussed at greater length in Chapter 8. Another advantage of the grog-clay mixture that has some bearing on our present problem is its interesting textural possibilities. The porosity and sparkle caused by the small particles of fired clay give it an inherent life.

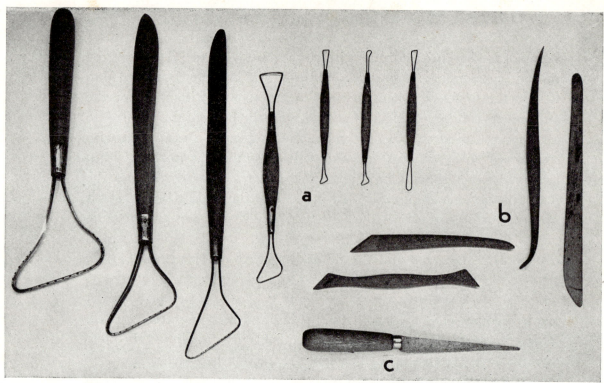

20

Modeling Tools

Before starting a new technique, let us look for a moment at some clay modeling tools. They are very simple, being designed for either pressing bits of clay into place (as in Figures 5 and 6) or for cutting off excess clay. The wire-end tools, (a) in Figure 20, are for this latter purpose. The wire loops are made of steel or brass, and the size varies with the kind of form it is used on as well as with the size of the piece. In almost every case it is preferable to use the largest tool that can be handled easily since a small one invites finickiness and whittling. The spatula-like boxwood shapes (b) are little more than adjuncts to the fingers. They are particularly useful for getting into small places and for texturing. A knife is convenient for slicing off large amounts of clay when broad changes are being made. Any kind of large-bladed knife will do; the one illustrated (c) is especially designed for clay and is called a fettling knife. (See Appendix 2 for sources of supply of tools and materials.)

Slab Construction

Now we are ready to develop a new technique. We will make a flexible slab which can be formed with the hands into the core of a design. The slab is made in the following manner: cover the wedging board with a piece of thin cotton cloth, tacking it at the corners with thumbtacks so that it is taut and free of wrinkles. On this, place two narrow strips of wood ½ inch, or a little less, in thickness, so that the space between them is about eight or ten inches. Fill this area with grog-clay slabs about one inch thick, cut on the wedging board wire. Knead them together, trying not to trap air. Then with a rolling pin, or some similar cylindrical object, roll the clay down until it is even with the wooden strips. You now have a tightly compressed slab, consistent in thickness but irregular in shape. Suppose the design you want to achieve is similar to that in Figures 22 or 23. Approximate the necessary width and height, allowing for the bending and forming. Tend toward oversize now, since it is easier to cut off than to add to the height and width. When the size and shape have been decided and drawn lightly on the slab, cut through with a knife at right angles and remove the excess clay.

If necessary, additional support can be given to the slab by a simple armature. For this particular problem, a ¼-inch wooden rod or dowel, slightly shorter than the height of the design, can be fastened to the modeling board by drilling a hole the exact size of the dowel. You must be careful that it is fastened at the proper angles, and remember that there are two different angles involved, front and side. By determining the direction of the axis of the total design, you can find these angles and drill the hole accordingly. With the dowel in place, lift the slab from the cloth, holding it in both hands and set it up around the armature. Care must be taken to keep the clay from slipping or falling, and you may have to build extra clay supports in places. Shape the slab slowly by bending and turning; it is all right to push the clay a bit now, but be careful not to break it or lose any of the thickness. Some additional cutting may be necessary to get the basis for the design. Work slowly, because the clay has to become rather hard before it is safe to do much modeling. It may have to be left alone to dry out for

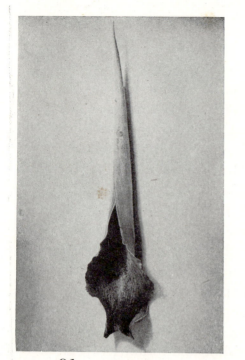

21

22

23

24

several hours in order to strengthen the structure and prevent sagging.

Once the slab is sufficiently hard to be sturdy, you can begin the final shaping. Drastic changes cannot be made, but parts of the slab can still be cut away. Most of the shaping at this stage should consist of surface modeling, of developing smaller planes, and of making minor adjustments of form. In general, the slab idea should be retained throughout, and only slight variations in thickness should be made where necessary for design purposes. With a little experimentation, the textural advantages of the grog-clay mixture become obvious. Try various methods of applying the clay, using the fingers, wooden modeling tools, and metal spatulas. Deviating from the modeling technique, scrape lightly over a surface with the wire-end tool and an interesting scratched texture will result; unless care is used, this can easily be overdone. If the slab becomes hard before the modeling is finished, the surface must be softened by brushing or spraying with water. However, this too, must be done with caution; too much water will cause the entire slab to become soft and in danger of collapsing. It is best to dampen only a small area at a time, being careful to remove from the modeling board excess water that would weaken the supporting sections.

We have a choice of two clay techniques now. In deciding which to use for a specific problem, you must consider the possibilities and limitations of each. The modeling technique is freer and is adaptable to most form ideas, especially those with massive proportions (Figures 25 and 27); the slab method can be used to exploit the other extreme of clay possibilities, such as the relatively thin sheet-like forms in Figures 26 and 28.

Color

The polychromatic use of color in sculpture has been employed with varying degrees of emphasis in nearly all periods of history. Most Greek sculptures, particularly the marbles, were elaborately painted. During the last few centuries there have been attempts at synthesizing color and three-dimensional shape relationships, most of which were

25

26

27

28

unsuccessful. The use of color increases the sculptural problems, and yet the temptation to try it is persistent because nature itself is so colorful.

If color is to be used successfully, it must be planned from the beginning and not applied as an afterthought when the design is finished. The concept of handling color in a three-dimensional form is necessarily different from that involved in painting. The use of color as a device for spatial illusion within a form is not only superfluous but works against one of the most important expressive characteristics of sculpture—its perceptual actuality in space. If illusionistic planes are introduced to the form and if there is a feeling that they are not actually where they seem to be, much of this expression of *being* is lost. Nor should one, in abstracting from nature, attempt to copy her color relationships. She has her own reasons for using those particular colors; if we understand them, well and good, but our purposes are not the same as hers. The green in a leaf, for instance, serves a biological function in the life of a tree, but in our use of the color we are primarily concerned with its psychological significance of coolness or its association with a particular mood. Color in sculpture may enrich the expressive possibilities of the form but it should not be used at the expense of the perceptual spatial unity of the design.

Unifying color relationships with those of planes, lines, and textures presents a more difficult problem than if the form is made of a uniform color. At this stage of development, you should take an experimental attitude toward color, limiting its use to contrast between planes. You should not break up a plane into various colors but use color wherever necessary to enrich or clarify the pattern of light and dark. An abrupt change in direction may also involve a change in color. In other words, you should try to use color to express more clearly the true spatial relationships of planes or masses. To help attain unity, simple color schemes should be used, such as several tones of one color or several closely related colors of the same tone. Generally, subdued colors are preferable, being more clay-like and easier to unify.

Most clays fire to a buff or reddish color. Low-fire colored clays can be bought or regular modeling clays can be colored by adding various oxides. The method of mixing these colored clays is described in

Chapter 8 (pages 89-93), along with the very important testing for shrinkage and final color.

One method of constructing polychromatic forms in clay is to complete the modeling and paint the design with colored slips—that is, clays containing coloring oxides which fire to various colors—thinned with water to the consistency of heavy cream. While this can be done quickly, the results are seldom satisfactory; the painting usually destroys subtle modeling and textures, and in most cases there is a lack of unity between shapes and color since they are arrived at separately. A better system is as follows: Study the range of colors which are available and select the mixtures that seem most appropriate to the kind of design you wish to achieve. Work out the form in colored drawings until you have a clear concept of the color arrangement. Make a rough sketch in clay keeping the color pattern in mind. Then, start the final design, building it in ordinary modeling clay until you are near the final surface. At this stage begin modeling with your colored clay. Care must be taken to keep the different colors from getting mixed. In this method the final shapes and textures are actually modeled in color and a greater synthesis can be attained. The designs in Figures 22, 27 and 28 were constructed in this manner.

Summary

By now we should have a much clearer understanding of the creative process. We have begun the process of transforming our reactions to nature into tangible form. Our finished problems will not be great works of art, but like the foliage of a plant, they will enable our roots to grow deeper and eventually bear fruit. In this chapter we have again experienced the interdependency of idea, form, and technical means. The technique of slab building opened new possibilities of abstracting nature, and the visual symbols obtained from our subject matter furnished the inspiration for our clay forms. We have found, also, at least part of the artist's function in society: through his creation of new visual abstractions, he contributes a freshness to the accepted, conventional symbols of his time, and thereby enriches the lives of his fellow men.

Progress in sculpture is a matter of expanding that on which we have already touched, probing deeper into nature and ourselves and expressing more and more through the symbols we abstract. We will learn other techniques, investigate many sources of ideas, both from within and without ourselves, and work in various materials; but always our sculptural problems will be a search for inspiration, clearer concepts, and ways of expressing them effectively in the third dimension.

5· Direct Building in Plaster

HAVING now had some experience with the synthesizing of idea and form with clay, let us turn our attention to another technique and material—direct building in plaster. Most plaster sculptures are cast from a mold—a process we will discuss at length in later chapters. This is an indirect method of working in which the original form is made in clay or some other material and then transferred to plaster. Direct building in plaster helps us to be more aware of the final material and its relationship to form and idea as the sculpture develops. The process is a simple one and easily controlled if the properties of the material and character of the technique are kept in mind; otherwise many difficulties may develop, such as uncontrolled form, breaks, protruding armatures, and hard and soft spots in the plaster. Before beginning, we will profit by a general investigation of the nature of plaster and why certain things happen as we work with it.

Varieties of Plaster

Plaster is made by heating naturally occurring gypsum rock, under controlled conditions, to drive off some of its water of crystallization ($CaSO_4 \cdot 2H_2O$ to $CaSO_4 \cdot \frac{1}{2}H_2O$). The resulting dry powder, which is the plaster we start with, can be recrystallized back to hydrated rock form by mixing with the proper amount of water. This period of rehydration, or setting, takes about half an hour, but it may be hastened or prolonged by the use of "accelerators" or "retarders," the simplest of which are hot water to speed the setting or cold water to slow it.

There are several kinds of plaster manufactured, all having the same basic properties but resulting in finished materials of varying characteristics. Some set harder, become more porous, or expand less than others, due to control of variations in the character of the plaster crystals during the calcining process. These types of plasters are classified according to the amount of water necessary to transform them into a fluid slurry of workable consistency. Chemically, only 18.6 pounds of water are needed to convert 100 pounds of plaster to set material, but, among the different types of plasters, from 30 to 70 pounds of water may be required to produce a mixture of proper thinness. The water in excess of the 18.6:100 ratio holds the particles apart and results in a more or less porous mass. It follows, then, that the less water required for a workable mix, the harder and more dense the set material will be; and the more water required, the softer and more porous the material will become. The advantages in each of these will be discussed further in the chapters on molding and casting.

Since exposure to moisture and age will render dry plaster unfit for use, it is best to keep on hand only the amount that will be used in a few weeks. For general studio use, regular molding plaster is the most satisfactory. Other kinds of plaster, such as the hard Hydrocals and Hydrostone, should be purchased only when needed for a special job. Molding plaster requires a relatively high ratio of water for mixing, but its hardness can be increased by reducing this amount of water slightly or by the addition of from 1 to 2 percent of dextrin, by weight, to the dry plaster. The structural strength can also be greatly increased if hemp fiber or other internal reinforcements are used.

29

30

31

32

Mixing Molding Plaster

The following directions are specifically for the mixing of molding plaster, but they apply also to the other plasters with the exception of the proportion of water used.

Clean water, equaling about two thirds of the desired volume of mixed plaster, is poured into a flexible container, such as a spun brass or rubber bowl. Into this, sprinkle rapidly as much plaster as will sink into the water, being careful to crush or remove lumps. When the plaster begins to pile up and no pools of water are left around the edges, we have a "normal mix" or approximately the 70:100 ratio mentioned above (Figure 29). If you wish to be more accurate, the amounts of water and plaster can be weighed, in which case 1 pound, 7 ounces of plaster is mixed with each pound of water.

This normal mix will yield a set plaster with a dry compressive strength of 2000 pounds per square inch, a dry density of 69 pounds per cubic foot, and an absorption power of 52.5 percent of its dry weight. If we add additional plaster the strength and density will increase and the absorption will drop, and, conversely, if we use less plaster, strength and density will decrease and absorption will be greater. However, there are limitations to the degree to which you can adjust the proportion; too much plaster will make the mixture too thick to stir thoroughly and too difficult to handle, while too little plaster will result in a weak mass when set.

When the plaster becomes wet and no "dry hills" are left, a matter of one or two minutes, the mixture is stirred to an even consistency. This is done best by spreading the fingers, flattening the palm as close as possible to the bottom of the container, and moving the hand rapidly from side to side. This will cause a flow of the mix from top to bottom and most of the air bubbles will rise to the top and break (Figure 30). With small containers, thorough stirring and a little vibration will perform the same function, but less efficiently.

The mixture of plaster has now begun the process of recrystallization back to its original form. For convenience in discussion we will divide this setting period into three phases: (1) the liquid stage when the mixture is fluid and can be poured and hemp fiber or burlap for reinforcement can be saturated with it (Figure 31); (2) the plastic stage (Figure 32), starting about fifteen minutes after the mix is stirred, during which the plaster can be modeled very much like clay; and (3) the hardening stage, occurring from the time the plaster is no longer plastic and lasting until the heat of recrystallization begins to warm the plaster. During this stage the plaster can be trimmed easily with a knife.

After the initial stirring, no additional plaster or water can be added; and once the mixture reaches the hardening stage, the set should not be broken by agitation or vibration. If this is done, the final plaster will be weak or fractured. Complete setting of plaster is indicated by its release of heat of crystallization, which occurs from thirty to forty minutes after mixing. After this the plaster can be handled quite freely, but its maximum strength is not reached until the free water has evaporated.

Plaster Tools

Which tools to use in working with plaster is a matter of personal preference. Certainly all those shown in Figure 33 are not necessary for the average problem. The groups are: (a) spatulas, (b) plaster knife, (c) large curved scrapers, (d) small tooth scrapers, and (e) rasps. These tools are of high-grade steel and should be kept free of caked plaster which causes them to rust. The spatulas are used for modeling plaster. Some of them are flexible and others are rigid. Those with flat ends are useful also as scrapers or cutting tools and are used mostly before the plaster gets hard. The knife is used between the plastic and hard stages for removing large amounts of excess plaster. The tooth scrapers and rasps are used after the plaster is hard for leveling planes and texturing.

Designing for the Built-up Plaster Technique

In this problem, we will pay particular attention to exploiting the possibilities of building with plaster. The reinforced plaster will be quite strong, and you should take advantage of the opportunity of using attenuated shapes and incorporating a large amount of space in the

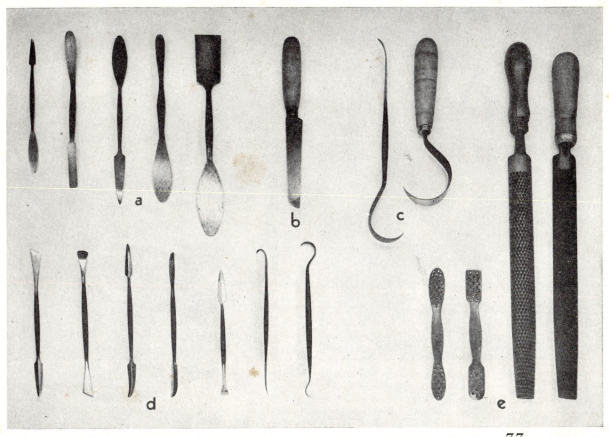

33

design. Since you will use a metal supporting structure (called an armature), relatively heavy masses can be supported by thin shapes. The plaster will be built up by modeling and worked down by cutting and filing, so that more precision of surface and edge can be obtained. In general, the design to be achieved should be expressive of light but strong reinforced shapes, and the subject matter should be an idea that lends itself to this kind of form.

Because of the difficulty of making changes in the set plaster, it is necessary to have a clear concept of the design before starting to work. A small sketch of soft wire and clay can be made to indicate the proportions, movements, and balance. Paper or cardboard may be preferable to clay for sketches of designs with thin flat shapes. In other cases, it may be best to work out the form with diagrammatic drawings instead of making a three-dimensional sketch.

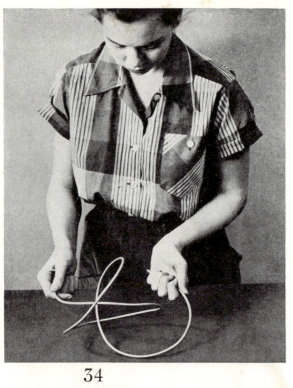

34

35

36

37

The Armature

Aluminum, copper, or iron wire or rods are used for the armature. This armature should be carefully planned because most of the structural strength of the model will depend upon it. The size and hardness of the wire will depend on the diameter of the thinnest section of the plaster and the character of the axes of the shapes. If most of the bends are simple and angular, a hard wire will be best, but if there are complicated curves, softer wire should be used. Whenever possible, joints should be welded or tied snugly with thinner wire. Iron armatures must be coated with shellac or lacquer to prevent rusting.

In Figure 34, the armature being bent into shape is of ¼-inch soft aluminum wire. The two ends were welded using a gas-compressed air torch and aluminum welding rod. This makes a relatively strong support for the plaster form (Figure 35).

The Building Procedure

A small amount of plaster is prepared, and by using a little more plaster than in a normal mix, a good hardness is assured. You should not mix more than can be used in half an hour; this is usually about half the amount of your first guess. While this is in the liquid stage, thin strands of hemp fiber are dipped in the bowl and covered with plaster. These are wound around the armature to strengthen the structure by making a stronger joint between the plaster and the metal (Figure 36). If there are to be large masses in the design, pads of fiber dipped in plaster will speed up the building process. Care should be taken that the fiber does not protrude to the surface of the form since it is hard to cut off.

If the plaster reaches the plastic stage before the winding of the strands of fiber is completed, it is best to leave the winding and model on the remaining plaster. Later, another small batch of plaster is mixed, and this process is repeated until the entire armature is covered with fiber.

For most of the work now, you will need plaster in the plastic stage, so your next mix can be made with warm water, to speed up the set-

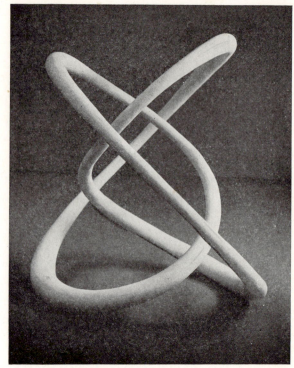

38   39

ting. It is futile to try modeling with liquid plaster. The ten to fifteen minutes necessary for the mix to reach the plastic stage can be spent trimming up the roughly modeled areas with a knife or rasp to help prevent overbuilding. During this stage of building, it is good practice to mix two small batches of plaster at a time, one with warm water and one with cold water. The warm-water mix will become plastic first, and by the time it is used up the cold-water mix will be almost ready to use for modeling. In this way some of the waiting between mixes is eliminated and the building progresses more rapidly.

Unlike clay, plaster is quite difficult to model with the fingers. Instead, a steel spatula such as that shown in Figure 37 should be used. As the final shapes develop, the technique becomes more and more a process of building up and cutting down. A plaster rasp which grates off the material is best for cutting; and to prevent breakage, strain on the thin sections should be avoided by supporting the piece as much as possible (Figure 38).

56

40   41

This process of adding and cutting away plaster can be continued over an indefinite period of time. However, fresh plaster should not be added to a form that has lost much of its free water without wetting the dry plaster. On small pieces, it is wise to saturate the form with water before starting to model again. When fresh plaster is added to a dry model, one of two things happens. If the new plaster is in the liquid stage and the old plaster is very dry, so much of the mixing water will be drawn off that complete recrystallization will not take place and the new plaster will be very weak. Or, if the new mix has reached the plastic stage before being added, the excess water, which normally makes the plaster porous, is absorbed before the plaster sets and the result is a very hard, dark, and sometimes glassy area. One of the ways of preventing this condition is discussed later in Chapter 12 (page 157), but for the plaster-building method it is best to keep the model wet while working on it.

If the plaster is cracked, it can be patched by cutting away the frac-

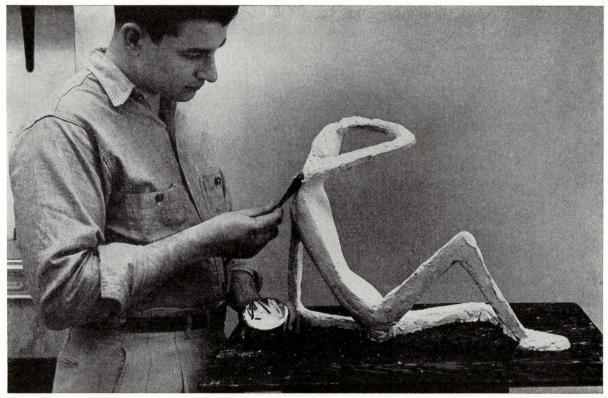

42

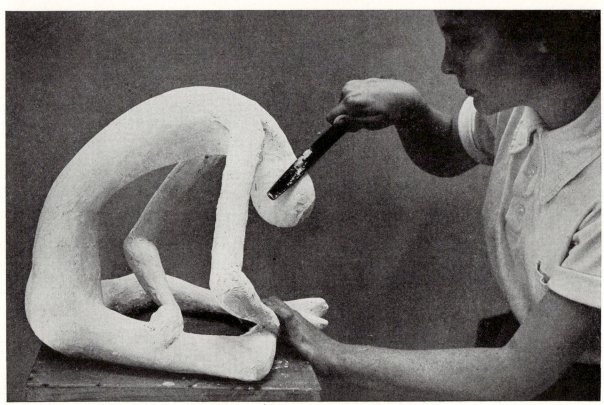

43

tured area and filling with plastic plaster. This should be done at a time when the piece can be left alone long enough for the patch to set completely.

Compare the designs in Figures 39, 40, and 41 with the previous clay problems and note to what extent the material and technique have controlled the form. It is interesting to imagine what would have happened if we had reversed the materials—that is, if we had used clay instead of plaster in these designs and plaster in place of clay in the former. You might think offhand that the clay designs would simply have been thinner and the plaster forms heavier, but further consideration should indicate that we would have two new sets of designs, entirely different from those illustrated.

Of course, the degree to which the nature of the plaster-building technique determines the form can be controlled. In many instances, a sculptor may conceive of his final sculpture in metal or cast stone and use the plaster-building technique as a convenient method of arriving at his desired form. This is also true of clay, though direct building in plaster eliminates the task of casting the clay into plaster. However, even if our conception is of a metal form, whether we construct it in clay or plaster will have a great deal to do with the final result. It seems as though our subconscious mind enters into an intrigue with characteristics of the immediate technique to influence our conscious efforts. While the two designs in Figures 42 and 43 are metal concepts, it is obvious that the plaster technique is playing a large part in determining the forms.

6· Constructions

SCULPTURE is usually divided into two groups, modeled and carved, but recently considerable interest has been turned to constructed form. While this is not a twentieth-century innovation, examples being found as far back as early Egyptian cultures, emphasis is today being placed on it as a sculptural form. Essentially, constructions are closer to the modeled than to the carved form, in that the design is built up and has few of the restrictions of carving from a block. On the other hand, the parts with which the constructions are made are sometimes carved.

Construction frees the sculptor from many of the problems of modeling and carving and offers him greater opportunities of combining materials and exploring spatial relationships. Some constructions, called mobiles, are designed to actually move through space, in a striving for a stronger expression of abstracted energy.

Our particular interest in this type of form will be to exploit the characteristics of the materials used. We will look for ideas that can best be expressed in given materials and forms that will express both the ideas and the materials. To do this we must have a knowledge of the substance being used—not necessarily a scientific knowledge but an intuitive understanding, a feeling for the material. Developing this kind of knowledge takes not just experience but a sensitive consideration for the material and plain common sense.

Material Potentialities

Materials have certain potentialities which can be utilized through various techniques. In Chapter 4 we found that by pressing clay into a slab we produced a piece of material with somewhat different characteristics from the original clay. In other words, we released latent properties when we shaped the clay into a flat sheet and curved the slab so that it supported its own weight. Similarly, a sheet of paper can be curved horizontally or vertically but not in both dimensions simultaneously. However, if a series of parallel cuts are made inside the sheet, it can be bent into complex curves. By this simple technique we have altered the character of the original sheet better to serve a purpose. Among other things, in this chapter we are going to investigate this aspect of materials and techniques. We will look for sculptural possibilities in the material, those properties which lend themselves to visual expression such as shaping, texturing, and coloring. Then we will find techniques for exploiting these characteristics to the fullest.

We will call the forms resulting from these experiments *constructions,* using the word loosely, since some of the designs will be made with only one piece of material. The only way to discover these sculptural potentials is through actually working with the material experimentally. Spend a few minutes bending, hammering, and joining pieces of sheet metal and you will learn many significant facts about the material which cannot be told to you. Thus, the following information is presented as a starter rather than as complete data on the materials.

We will begin with sheet metal simply because its sculptural potential is greater and more obvious than other materials discussed in this chapter. Of the variety available we will select three to discuss here, aluminum, copper, and lead. Though similar in many respects, each possesses characteristics that distinguish it from the others sculpturally, and the techniques of handling and consequent form will vary accordingly.

Aluminum Sheet

Aluminum is a white metal, relatively strong in relation to its light weight. The sheet stock ranges in thickness from $\frac{1}{16}$ to $\frac{1}{8}$ inch and is easily cut with a hacksaw, jigsaw, or shears. The surface can be filed or sanded but it is difficult to polish. Some sheet stock is given an anodic treatment, called Alumilite finish, which produces a high sheen, but if this coating is sanded the polish is lost.

Sheets are manufactured by rolling the cold metal under great pressure until the desired thickness is attained. This strain causes molecular changes in the structure of the metal which produces a condition known as "work hardened." The sheets become very hard and brittle and will eventually fracture unless softened. The softening process is known as "annealing" and consists simply of heating the sheet until the molecular strains are released and the metal again becomes pliable. The amount of strain left in the sheet determines its properties of hardness, softness, springiness, or pliability. The surface finish of the last set of rollers through which the sheet passes determines its surface quality.

Aluminum sheet, as it is bought, possesses a variety of properties. For forms with flowing curved planes a hard, or "tempered," sheet is needed, since the strains in the metal help it to take on a flowing character. If you bend a hard aluminum sheet at a sharp angle you impart additional strain to the metal and it may fracture. Certainly it will if the bend is flattened and the sheet bent again in the same area. In order to make sharp bends safely we should buy softer stock or soften the hard metal by heating it. Aluminum melts at a relatively low temperature without perceptibly changing color, so experiment with a scrap piece of the same metal to see just how much heat the sheet will take before melting.

The easiest and usually most satisfactory way to join aluminum is with rivets. Holes of the proper size can be punched or drilled and the

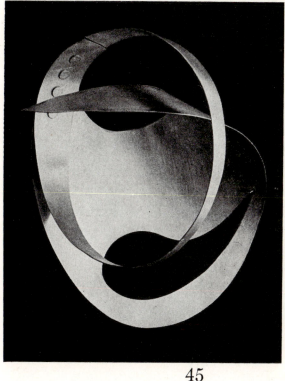

44　　　　　　　　　　　　　　　45

rivets tightened with a small iron bar called a rivet set. Sometimes it is best to emphasize the joint rather than to hide it. The structural strength implicit in a well-made joint may add to the expression of the design. There is a solder made especially for joining aluminum but it lacks strength and is difficult to use. Thicker aluminum stock such as wire or rods can be welded, but this demands considerable skill and practice and is impossible with thin sheets.

Figure 44 shows a design formed by making two L-shaped cuts in a triangular piece of soft sheet aluminum. By carefully planned bending, an interesting spatial organization resulted, unified both structurally and visually. In Figure 45, the form is derived to a large extent by exerting pressure against the resistance to bending of harder tempered aluminum. The character of the resulting curves is determined by the consistency of the stresses within the metal, the manner in which the sheet is cut, and the quality and quantity of the force exerted on it. When this pressure is fixed by joining, the result is a visual expression of forces working in harmony.

46   47

Copper Sheet

Like aluminum, copper is available in a number of thicknesses and various hardnesses. It can be polished to a high luster or can be colored with acids or heat. The melting point is quite high and it is easily joined with lead-tin solder or by brazing with silver or brass rods, although, as with aluminum, rivets may be preferable in many cases.

If you place a piece of soft copper on a hard surface such as an anvil and beat it with the round end of a hammer that area of the metal is slightly stretched and work-hardened. Beating in a circular pattern will cause the edges of the piece to rise and by controlling the force of the blows you can control the resulting shape. Some of the energy of the hammering is retained as strains and stresses are set up within the material. In Figures 46 and 47 the soft pliable copper has been transformed into a strong, tense substance through the very process of shaping. The metal has become harder and the structural strength of the sheet has been greatly increased by the use of reverse curves.

64

48

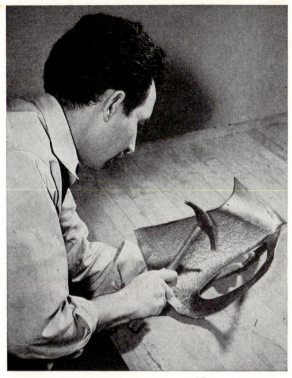

49

50

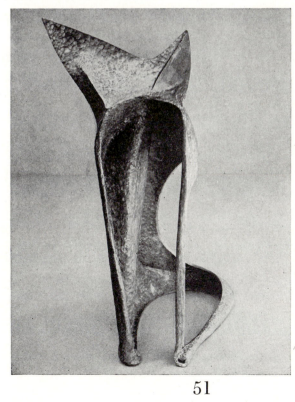

51

The concept of the dancers is expressed not only through the dynamic rhythms of the organization but by the fusion of the form character and tenseness of the material with this organization.

Hammered Lead

Lead is a very soft metal which lends itself readily to the "hammered-out" form. Its molecular structure is such that very little work-hardening takes place. A thick section can be stretched into a much larger thinner area by beating. In the case of copper, the force exerted by the hammer was transformed into hardness with little loss of thickness, but in hammering lead the material "gives in" and there is a noticeable flow of metal as it is beaten. In other words, the copper, through its absorption of the energy applied to it, aided in determining the character of the form, while the shaping of the lead depends more on the will of the sculptor.

You should have a pretty clear concept of what is wanted of the lead before beginning. A small model in clay, and a working drawing which makes allowances for the stretching of the lead, are helpful. The sheet of lead, ⅛ inch thick for most small problems, can be cut with shears or a jigsaw (Figure 48). The basic shaping is done with the hands, aided in places by beating the metal a little to stretch it (Figure 49). When the general form is established as in Figure 50, some trimming with the shears may be necessary before continuing. The final shaping of the form will take considerable time, but the lead will respond readily to willful handling (Figure 51). Textures can be varied by the use of hammers with smaller or larger heads, by scraping to smooth, and by burnishing to polish. The lead can be cleaned with acetic acid or vinegar and darkened with hydrochloric acid.

Direct Modeling with Metal

While constructions free us of many of the problems of modeling, we miss the advantages of subtlety. Even hammered metal does not give us much opportunity to build up and vary the thickness of shapes. Contemporary tools and materials, such as oxyacetylene welding and cutting torches and low-melting metal alloys, make it possible for sculptors to build directly in metal. The technique has advantages of both construction and modeling. Shapes can be cut from thick sheets of metal, brazed or welded together, and modeled over by fusing bits of metal to the form.

Some metal alloys melt at very low temperatures, making it possible to build up a form with a soldering iron. One of these is Wood's metal, which is sold commercially as Cerrobend. This remarkable metal, an alloy of bismuth, lead, tin, and cadmium, melts at 158° F, only 38 percent of the temperature necessary to melt its lowest melting component, tin. It has a tensile strength of 5990 pounds per square inch and a Brinell hardness of 9.2 which is over twice that of lead. Thin bars can be made by melting the Cerrobend in the top part of a double boiler (or by some other controlled heat) and by pouring it on a sheet of corrugated cardboard. This metal can then be built up on a clean lead, copper, or brass armature by slight heating. A thermostatically controlled soldering iron is preferable for the modeling since too much heat will cause some of the previously added metal to come off. Another similar alloy, requiring slightly more heat to handle, is Cerromatrix, which melts at 250° F.

Modalloy is the trade name of a low-fusing metal which is available in sheet form. The recommended technique for its use is to crumple up the sheets and compress them around an armature. The final surface is worked over with a heated tool to fuse the metal.

Building with Solder

A simple introductory technique for direct modeling in metal is shown in Figures 52-55. With a clear idea in mind, the basic shape is cut out of clean sheet metal and bent into its proper position (Figure 52). In this problem, tempered sheet brass (70 percent copper, 30 percent tin) $\frac{1}{16}$ inch thick was used. Next, strips of lead, the size and shape of the heavier built-up areas, are cut and cleaned by brushing with acetic acid or by filing. These strips are added to the brass by first coating the surfaces of the joint, both the brass and the lead, with solder. This process is called tinning and is done in the following

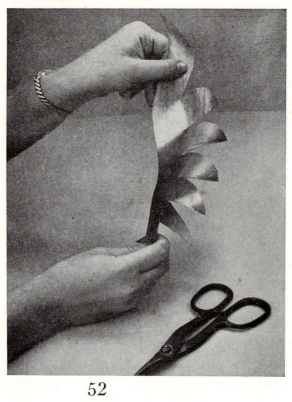

52

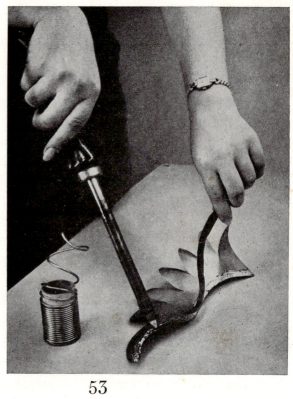

53

54

55

manner: the end of the soldering iron is cleaned and coated with solder by rubbing the four beveled surfaces in a small pool of melted solder and flux. Solder can be bought as wire with a hollow, flux-filled center. Fluxes are of three kinds: rosin, paste, and acid; the latter is preferable since it is easier to remove from the finished work. Place one of the solder-coated planes of the iron against the metal and rub vigorously, adding small amounts of solder and flux until the surface has a thin coating. When both surfaces are tinned, they are put together and heated with the tip of the iron and additional melted solder allowed to run in between (Figure 53).

When the lead strips have been joined, the areas can be filled in and modeled over with the solder (Figure 54). It is important that the surface of the brass and lead be well tinned before building up. With a little practice, modeling with solder can be very sensitive. The hot iron, pushed against the form, will remove solder and level off the planes. A coarse file or rasp is helpful where more precision is needed.

The finished sculpture should be cleaned with soap and water to remove the acid flux. Interesting color effects are gotten by brushing the piece with acid solutions. One part sulphuric acid, 1 part copper sulphate, and 5 parts water mixed into a solution and brushed on the solder will produce a grayish green with bits of red copper deposited in the crevices. This piece, Figure 55, was first brushed with acetic acid to clean both the brass and the solder and washed thoroughly. A half-and-half mixture of hydrochloric acid and water heated to 200° F was brushed freely over the solder and a small amount of copper oxide was worked over the moist surface. More of the hot solution and oxide were added until the solder became quite black. Washed with water and rubbed down with a soft cloth the color became rich brown and gray. The polished brass areas were rubbed with steel wool.

Plastic

The history of plastics, which begins about 1850, is a history of the search for substitutes, first for ivory, then for hard rubber, and later for such things as leather, amber, glass, tortoise shell, etc. The stigma of "inferior substitute" has followed the word *plastic* right up to the present, even though the industry has produced dozens of entirely new materials with potentials transcending the uses to which they are put. Perhaps one reason we persist in thinking of plastics as cheap material is because they are so badly misused; little of their latent beauty is ever seen. Industrially, no plastic form—that is, no form expressive of the nature of the substance as metal form is expressive of metal—has evolved as yet, and as long as designers are content to use plastics as substitute materials, their beauty will remain hidden. Our purpose here is to explore some of the visually expressive possibilities of one group of the many kinds of plastic on the market. (Others will be discussed in the section on plastic casting in Chapter 15.) The one selected here is the transparent thermoplastic made from acrylic resins. It is available in both rods and sheets and is sold under the trade names Acryloid, Crystalite, Lucite, and Plexiglas.

This plastic can be worked with the same tools used for wood and metal: hand saw, jigsaw, drill press, files, etc. It is hard and brittle but becomes very pliable, comparable to gum rubber, when heated to 220° F to 300° F. For most bending of pieces up to ⅛ inch in thickness, submersion in boiling water softens the material sufficiently. For thicker material, a hot oil bath or an oven with controlled heat is necessary. When the plastic cools to atmospheric temperature it will retain the shape into which it was bent.

One of the most outstanding properties of acrylic materials is the ability to "pipe" light. The following explanation of this phenomenon, while not the whole story, is adequate for our purposes. The light, entering an edge or end of a piece of this material, is reflected back and forth by the polished surfaces until it reaches the opposite edge. The rays of light in the plastic advance lengthwise, rebounding between the polished sides, and will not escape provided the sheet or rod is not bent more than 47.8° or curved on a radius less than three times the thickness of the material. For instance, a ¼-inch rod may be bent to a radius as small as ¾ inch, or a sheet may be bent at any angle up to 47.8° without much leakage of light. By breaking the polish of one of the surfaces, we can allow some of the light to escape and this textured area becomes "lighted." This can be done by sanding, scratching, carving, etc., to produce different effects.

70

56

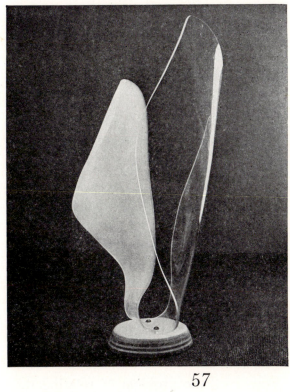

57

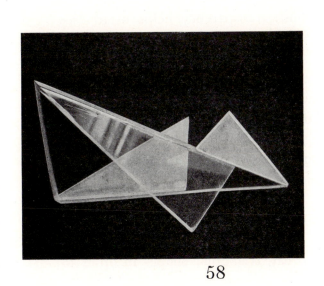

58

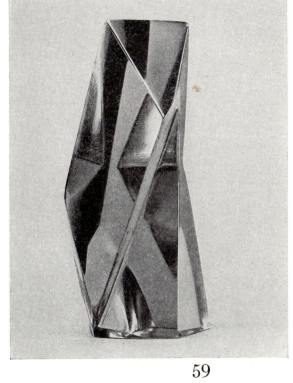

59

Figure 56 shows an experiment with this kind of edge-lighting. Variations in the thickness of the lighted edge were made by filing at an angle to produce a wider escape area for the light. The portion of plastic with polished surfaces is dematerialized, and the design is an organization of beams of light.

The two plastic designs in Figures 57 and 58 make greater use of transparency along with this edge lighting. Parts of the plastic were sandblasted to "paint" the planes with light. This technique of controlling mass and space through light within the design has many possibilities which should be explored in working with plastic. Qualities of transparency should be exploited, too; space seen through even the clearest plastic has a different quality from space seen through an open area or hole in the plastic.

Designing for Transparency

In the section on three-dimensional design (pages 8-10), we discussed the problem of relating the perception of two-dimensional views by repetition, rhythms, and other uses of planes, so that each view "spoke" of the same sculpture. With a transparent medium these views are not isolated visually; we can see nearly all the planes of the form from all positions. To some extent, transparency helps us to "see what we know is there." This is one reason why transparent plastic is such a fascinating material.

Since we see nearly all the planes all the time, in designing for transparency our planes should be fewer. Not only must shapes on each side be planned to go together, but they also have to be designed with the planes which are seen through them. Other shapes result from the overlapping of these planes, and all must be organized into a unified design. The carved plastic piece in Figure 59 shows how complex even a simple transparent form becomes. Planes are polished and bent in varying degrees to control the light. Some are emphasized; others are dematerialized. With so many variables involved in the form, all planes were simplified to flat, triangular shapes in order to unify the design.

Wood and Plywood

Wood has long been in use as a sculptural medium, primarily as a material for carving. Since a whole chapter is devoted later to carving, we will concern ourselves here with constructional aspects only. Most of us acquire some knowledge and feeling for wood in the process of growing up because it is so plentiful and is used in the making of so many kinds of objects. However, a few words about its structure and its possibilities and limitations in constructions should be in order.

Wood grain, which is discussed in more detail in Chapter 10, is the result of the annual growth rings, which are added one each year as the tree grows and develops a structure of more or less concentric cones. The pattern of grain that is seen in lumber is often called the figure. It results from a combination of the grain structure and the manner in which the tree trunk is cut into lumber. A board, for instance, may be plain-sawn, cut on a tangent to the growth rings, or quarter-sawn, cut from flat faces of quarters of the trunk. The rather striped pattern on the planes of the board is caused by the light portion of the growth ring, which is called spring wood, alternating with the darker, which is summer wood. Spring wood is made up of larger cells and is softer than summer wood. Each cone grows independently of the previous year's growth and is not joined strongly to it. Laterally, from edge to edge, there is much less strength than lengthwise or end to end.

The cells which make up the growth rings are called wood fibers. They are long in proportion to the thickness, grow vertically, and taper toward each end. Working with wood, one becomes aware of three distinct conditions of direction which are controlled by the particular position of these fibers: (1) *across the grain,* which is laterally across the annual rings, (2) *against the grain,* lengthwise and into the ends of the fibers, like rubbing hair in the "wrong" direction, and (3) *with the grain,* lengthwise and over the fibers. Since there is little bond between the cells of different growth rings, working across the grain tends to separate the layers and tear the wood. If one works against the grain, with a cutting edge, the position of the fibers causes the tool to be pulled deeper and deeper into the wood. Cutting and sanding should be done with the grain wherever possible.

The classification of woods into softwoods and hardwoods is misleading. Generally, the wood of all coniferous trees is called softwood even though some of it is much harder than wood from the broad-leaved trees which is called hardwood. The even grain and color which, as a rule, are typical of hardwoods make them preferable to softwoods.

Much of the structural strength of the trunk of the tree is lost when it is cut into boards. As mentioned above, there is little lateral strength and flexibility in thin boards. The development of plywood has overcome this weakness and produced a product of approximately equal strength and flexibility in all dimensions. More than that, plywood can be made in large thin sheets and the tendencies to warp and buckle are lessened. The plys of wood are made by revolving a log against a large blade which peels off layers corresponding roughly to annual rings. These are dried and glued together in such a manner that the grains of adjacent sheets run at right angles to each other. Almost invariably, plywood is made up of an odd number of sheets, and the two face plys are one half the thickness of the others. In this way the grains of the two faces run in the same direction and there is uniform strength and flexibility.

While plywood structure has been known for many years, recently developed methods of resin-bonding and pressure-forming have opened possibilities that were previously inconceivable. Actually, plywood has become more of a plastic than a wood form, and with modern techniques, compound curvatures and complex shapes can be made. Unfortunately, the equipment for handling molded plywood is too expensive for sculpture studios, but we may hope that some day the molded plywood technique will be available to sculptors. In the meantime, many of the inherent properties of plywood can be explored with the usual workshop equipment.

The Wood Form

Psychologically, we respond differently to each material. In many ways, we feel closer to wood than to metal or plastic, partly because of its obvious organic origin but also because of its physical warmth, both tactile and visual, its light weight, and its comforting fibrous strength. Like metal and plastic, it "asks" to be formed in harmony with its inner structure. As the tree grows, its will to survive builds its character; its resistance to natural forces—wind, cold, gravity—is developed. Visually, the tree's form tells the story of this struggle as a human's form is expressive of his life.

Driftwood tells another kind of story—the abrasive action of elements abnormal to the tree, water and sand, on, not the growing tree, but the substance-potential of its body which it developed while living. These fascinating forms express the resistance of the structure of wood to the gentle but persistent carving of nature. However, this is not sculpture; nature produces natural forms and humans produce sculpture.

Our design, then, does not have to resemble a tree, which has done an excellent job of manifesting itself, or a piece of driftwood, which nature has shaped for reasons of her own. But we can learn much about the character of wood from studying both tree and driftwood, and we may find inspiration for our own sculptural ideas in their shapes. However, to understand wood fully, we must work with it and feel its mild, condescending resistance to proper handling. We may abuse it and shape it in a way the structure of the material does not permit, but we cannot feel victorious; the wood will break, or, worse than that, refuse to look like wood.

Construction in Wood

When planning a design for wood construction, you should keep the following in mind: (1) the substance, wood, has a character which must be allowed to express itself; (2) the particular type of wood, board lumber or plywood, is wood plus or minus certain properties; and (3) in shaping this material to your will, you are limited by the tools and techniques you employ. A suggested problem to get started with actual construction follows:

1. Try to find or invent a shape idea which seems to be in harmony with wood.

2. Plan another shape, closely related to the former but smaller, and

75

60

61

62

space it inside the first shape so that the area between the two is well organized and interesting.

3. Draw this pattern on a piece of wood about ¾-inch thick, and cut out the two shapes on a jigsaw. A small hole drilled on the outline of the inner shape will make it possible to insert the saw blade there so as not to have to cut through the outer shape.

When the sawing is finished we will have *three* shapes—the two pieces of wood and the opening in the larger one. If a base is planned, there may be five shapes, as in the design shown in Figure 60. Next, study the possibilities of joining the two pieces, looking for opportunities of creating various relationships based on the principles of order. The edges of the wood can be beveled and turned by rasping and filing to create three-dimensional movements and rhythms.

The pieces should be finished as far as possible before joining. The design in Figure 60 was joined by two countersunk screws at the base and a short piece of ½-inch plastic rod toward the middle.

Construction in Plywood

The two properties of plywood which can best be explored in these problems are its particular kind of strength and the laminated structure of alternating grain. In designs emphasizing the former, thin shapes are possible as in Figure 61, where ¼-inch three-ply wood was used. The parts were joined with ¹⁄₁₆-inch dowels. The rhythmical flow of the lines in Figure 62 was attained by using two pieces of ¾-inch, thirteen-ply wood, and by beveling the edges into the sides and joining the pieces at the base.

Combining two or more materials in a design gives us the opportunity of opposing and contrasting their respective properties, besides offering a richer variety of color and texture. The string and plywood design (Figure 63) emphasizes the balance of the thrusts of the plywood parts and the tension of the string. Unity results from organizing the strings into transparent triangular planes and the use of similarity of shapes. In Figure 64 the metallic strength and flexibility is contrasted with the rigidness of the plywood. A stability results from the horizontal lines of the plys.

77

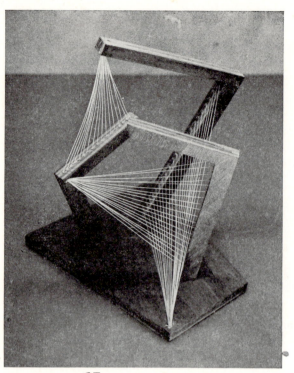

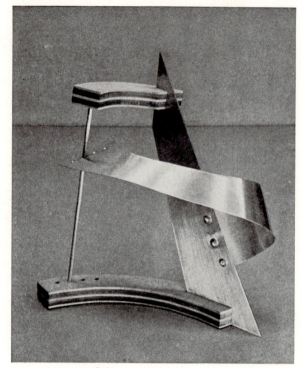

63   64

Summary

We will return to these materials in later chapters. In the meantime we will find it advantageous to sum up what has been learned from our experience with them thus far.

Each material has unique physical properties, a temperament, and a life of its own. When we select a piece of material for sculptural purposes we must enter into a tacit partnership with it; we must look for its sculptural potential, find out how to release it, and try to arrive at a form, not only acceptable to the material, but preferably, with the whole-hearted aid of the material.

7·The Study of the Figure

THE OLD SAYING that no two people see alike is probably true: no one sees clearly, objectively, and without prejudice. We see very little with our eyes—we actually see with the mind through a group of previously formed mental constructions.   Usually, what little our eyes perceive of an object is just sufficient to stimulate our idea of it.   For instance, we can recognize most of the objects around us at a glance and rightfully say we have *seen* them.   Looking at something which we have not seen before, we grasp rather easily that which fits into our idea world, but it is difficult and even painful to absorb visual perception to which we are unaccustomed.   We see what we want to see or have already seen, rejecting most, if not all, that is new to us.   So, most of the time, we go about thinking we are seeing a great deal, when we are actually only conjuring up previously formed ideas from our mental catalogue and allowing our perception to atrophy.

Learning to See

One can learn to see more clearly if a conscientious and systematic effort is put forth. We can train our eyes to perceive basic rather than superficial form, and, with perhaps more effort, we can open our minds to new visual stimuli. The key to the solution is to establish a situation in which we can force ourselves to see beneath the surface and find the underlying structure and basic relationships. Drawing from nature is one helpful method; modeling from life in the third dimension is another. Combining the two affords an opportunity of more complete perception and is less apt to allow us to drift back into stereotyped vision.

In earlier chapters, we made some elementary three-dimensional studies of nature, particularly inanimate form, but our purposes now necessitate a more complex form. We will study the human figure, partly because it is more practical for studio work, but primarily because we will be able to respond mimetically to the model—that is, take the pose ourselves and feel the structural relationships, the stresses and strains, in our bodies.

We must keep in mind that this is a study to help train our eyes to see and not a method of producing sculpture. The end-product is valueless except as an indication of our degree of success in perceiving and establishing the form of the model in clay. Most of what we will learn could be learned by simply walking around the model and studying the form, without modeling at all. The value of the figure we build is primarily that of note-taking; we put in it the relationships we have seen so that our minds will be freer to concentrate on further seeing. Of course, modeling technique and discipline will also be developed, but this is of secondary importance; once a form is seen clearly and held vividly in the mind, modeling it is a simple matter.

Studying the figure in this manner, we will not be interested in muscles as such but in the masses and shapes they assume. A knowledge of anatomy may or may not be helpful, depending on whether it can be subordinated to the problem of learning to see; if we cannot see the masses for the muscles, such knowledge will be harmful to an over-all concept of the figure.

larger element will come first; look for the over-all axis of the total form—that is, a single line running from the stand to the top of the model's head and passing through the center of the total mass. This line will have two aspects, front and profile, which are independent of each other except for height; if we look at the figure from the center of the front position of the stand, the axis may be a kind of S curve, while from the profile it may be angular. In other words, axes should be seen as three-dimensional lines. When this major axis is seen clearly, we will have a control for establishing the smaller axes and can begin to arrange the armature wires.

There is one point on a standing figure which is almost invariably on the vertical axis of the pose and also on a line through the center of gravity. This point is the pit of the neck. It should be established first on the armature, by bending the wires so that the main axis of the pose goes through both it and the armature support (which cannot be moved). Having fixed this point three-dimensionally, we retain it throughout the study, relating all other points and axes to it. For instance, in establishing the position of the ankles, an imaginary vertical line dropped from this point on the figure may be compared with a similar imaginary vertical line on the armature, and the position of the ankles established accordingly.

We should be sufficiently accurate in the arrangement of the armature that no shifting of the wires will be necessary after we begin building in clay. When we have arrived at this degree of accuracy, a clay foundation is built (Figure 66), anchoring the leg wires firmly to the modeling board. If this first stage seems long and drawn out, remember it is not merely preliminary work but actually what we set out to do—that is, we have been studying the figure.

Now we can begin closer study of the large basic shapes, looking beneath the surface planes for the structural core, the largest and simplest shape that fits within the mass. Visualizing this core as a geometric form will help in establishing it first in the mind and then in clay. For instance, the core of the hips may be seen as a rectangular box shape positioned in precise relationships to imaginary vertical and horizontal lines. As we begin to construct these masses, we follow the technique discussed in the earlier work with clay (Figure 67).

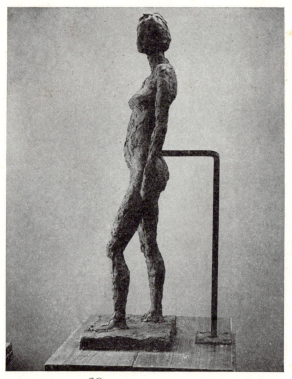

69

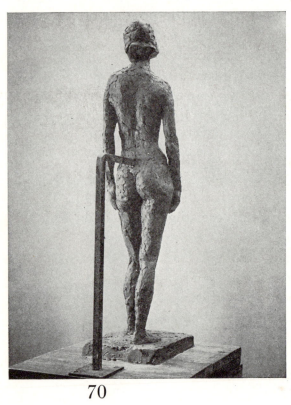

70

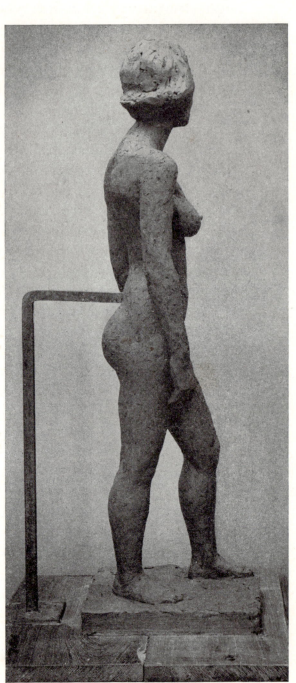

71

The following rules and suggestions may be helpful to beginners:

1. Separate the process into three parts: studying the figure, establishing certain findings in the mind, and building them in clay.

2. Study the figure from many different positions, always looking for big relationships first.

3. Continually check on large relationships, axes, and shapes.

4. Use the pit of the neck as a fixed point, relating points and lines to it.

5. Draw lines in the clay to indicate axes (Figure 68).

6. Use the planes of the model's stand as references to horizontal planes and directions.

7. Make corrections freely but do not move the armature wires. It is better to allow them to protrude if they are wrong.

8. Work three-dimensionally and evenly over the entire figure. Do not model outlines.

The stage of development shown in Figure 69 may be as far as we can get in three hours, but if it is reasonably accurate in its representation of the movement of axes in the posed model, the time has been well spent. The figure is not accurate in proportion because we have concentrated on axes and establishing a foundation. Figures 70 and 71 show further developments of shape and proportion. Once the large planes are found and established, the smaller ones fall into place rather easily as the shapes grow.

Throughout the study there will be some exaggeration; perhaps our enthusiasm in seeing movements and planes not usually seen causes extra emphasis to be put on them. This is not altogether undesirable, especially in the early stages, since most beginners tend to lose both movement and basic planes as the study develops. To offset this tendency toward stiffness in the later stages, a little exaggeration may be carried through right to the end of the study (Figure 71), although to see clearly, we should be conscious of our exaggeration.

Small shapes, such as the facial features, fingers, and toes are best handled sketchily in small studies and kept subordinated to larger planes. To study them properly, they should be made as separate studies and at least life-size.

This study is not a creative process in itself, nothing has been ex-

85

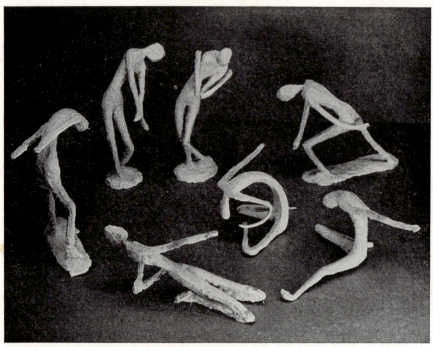

72

pressed, nothing imagined or designed, and the material was just a convenient substance to hold our visual perception. If there are individual differences in a group of studies, it simply means that complete objectivity in seeing is impossible. The "difference" between the clay study and the human model may be called expressive, but since our purpose was otherwise and the whole nature of the process at odds to the creative process, any expressiveness is necessarily negligible. However, problems of this kind sharpen our powers of perception and increase our knowledge of structure and our store of form ideas.

The plaster sketches in Figure 72 were made through a more creative approach. Instead of studying a posed model, the student experienced the action by assuming the position of the figure periodically during the construction in plaster. This method of studying the figure recalls a common experience, but one that is usually unconscious. In our minds, we continually construct three-dimensional images of ourselves so that we *know* what position our bodies are in without actually seeing them. Combining this mimetic study with the visual one strengthens our perception of form.

86

8· Terra Cotta Techniques

IN CHAPTERS 3 and 4 we learned the rudiments of two clay techniques: modeling and slab building. At that time only enough of the material characteristics and techniques were covered to satisfy the immediate problems. In this chapter, we will go more thoroughly into clay as a sculptural medium, extending our knowledge of the modeling technique and investigating methods of hollow construction.

Clay

Clays are natural earth materials. They are plastic in the raw state but permanently hard when fired above a red heat. After clay has been fired, it is usually called *terra cotta,* which means "cooked earth." Pure clay is called kaolinite and is the product of the decomposition of granite or other igneous rocks. Clays are classified into two groups: residual and sedimentary. Residual clays are found near the parent rock and are comparatively pure; sedimentary clays are those which have been deposited by water, wind, glaciers, etc. These are usually impure, having picked up foreign matter while being moved about. Pure clay consists of silica, alumina, and water in a state of combination, and forms the basis of all clays. Impurities such as organic matter, free silica, sand, calcium, magnesium, and mineral oxides are found in all sedimentary and most residual clays. These impurities determine the properties of porosity, fusibility, density, plasticity, and color in the different types of clays.

For modeling purposes, two types of sedimentary clays are particularly suitable: ball clay and shale. Ball clay is very plastic and, when a piece is pinched off, a thin trailing edge results. This high plasticity is referred to as "fatness." Ball clay is made up of very fine particles and retains its moisture much longer than other clays. This is an advantage in modeling when one works on a piece over a long period of time. It fires to a cream or light buff color, which indicates the presence of a small amount of iron oxide. There are two disadvantages to ball clay as a modeling medium: (1) its tendency to hold moisture, an advantage in the modeling stage, prolongs thorough drying before firing and sometimes results in warping and cracking; and (2) it lacks raw strength—that is, the ability to support its own weight in the plastic stage.

Shale, on the other hand, has somewhat opposite characteristics. It is composed of larger flat-shaped particles, and its plasticity is lower, causing a degree of brittleness. This condition is called "shortness." Shale is rather porous and dries rapidly but it has considerable raw strength. Most shale fires to a deep red color.

If we grant their disadvantages, either of these clays can be used successfully for modeling. Ideally, though, it is best to work out a mixture of ball clay and shale to suit the particular working conditions —a greater proportion of ball clay for dry atmospheres, more shale for thin, unsupported form, etc. For general modeling, a half-and-half mixture is completely satisfactory.

Most clays when bought are relatively dry, and water must be added. When being mixed, the clay should be slaked down in water and stirred to make a thick liquid, which is called slip. Unless the clay has been cleaned before, it must be screened through a sieve. Ball clay should be put through a 100-mesh screen and shale through an 80- to 100-mesh. Some of the water is then removed from the slip either by running it through a filter press or by pouring it onto a plaster board and leaving it until the proper consistency is reached. When the clays are plastic, the necessary quantities are weighed out and the two are wedged together. The wedging process was described in Chapter 4. This procedure is satisfactory for general modeling, but a more accurate method is to weigh out the amounts of each clay while dry, since ball clay and shale require different proportions of water to make them plastic. As the clay dries, the evaporating water often deposits salts on the surface. Various impurities in the clay or water that is mixed with it, such as calcium, sulphur, or magnesium, cause a whitish scum when the piece is fired. To prevent this, a small amount of barium carbonate, about 1 percent by weight, should be mixed with the clay. This can be done either in the slip or plastic stage, though mixing is easier in the former.

Color in natural clays is caused primarily by iron oxide, which fires red; pure clay fires white. We can control the color by the addition of other oxides. Manganese dioxide or copper oxide produce black; cobalt oxide, blue; chrome oxide, green; and uranium oxide, yellow. If the original clay fires white, any of these oxides added in amounts of about 5 percent by weight will produce a strong color. If the base clay fires orange or red it will, of course, be impossible to change it to a blue or green without adding an excessive amount of pigment, and this would tend to destroy the properties of the clay. As a rule, 10 percent of oxide is a maximum, especially if grog is also used in the mixture. The easiest method of combining the pigment and clay is to mix them together thoroughly while dry and wedge the clay considerably after it has been made plastic. However, it is also possible to wedge the color into plastic clay. If grog is used, the two can be wedged in simultaneously.

A wide color range can be made by combining various mixtures. Samples should be made and an accurate record kept of the ingredients and their proportions. The temperature to which the clay is fired is an important factor in the final color and should be marked on the back of the samples for future reference. The scum, mentioned above, often hides much of the richness of the clay's color, and barium carbonate should be added to all color mixtures, especially dark ones.

In the plastic state, most clay mixtures appear gray, regardless of the color they will be when fired. This can be confusing when working on a polychromatic design and often results in mistakes. A solution to the problem is to mix into plastic clay a ceramically inert pigment, such as charcoal, or any of the aniline or alizarin colors, which burn out without affecting the final color. In this way the mixes can be readily distinguished and the color pattern will be easier to design. Color tests should be made to be sure the added pigment does not change the fired color.

Some of the advantages of using grog in clay mixtures have already been discussed in Chapter 4. Besides its contributions to textural possibilities and stability in the raw state, grog cuts down on shrinkage and warpage, and, because of the porosity imparted to the clay, there is less danger of cracking during the drying-out and firing periods. This porosity also makes possible a technique of working that could not be used with ordinary clay. Since the small particles of fired clay give off and absorb water so readily, a mass can be built up, allowed to dry almost to the leather-hard stage, and then the modeling can be continued. The purpose in doing this is to develop a hard, strong core which will help support the clay that is built onto it. Care should be taken not to let the clay get too hard and to make a good joint between the hard and soft clay. The surface of the core should be scratched with a pointed tool and brushed with water until sticky before modeling onto it. When the softer clay is worked firmly into the softened surface, the two consistencies will equalize quickly, resulting in a strong joint. As soon as this is accomplished, modeling can continue quite freely. Grog, then, adds to the physical strength of a modeled form in two ways: it makes the raw clay stronger, and it allows working after the clay has hardened considerably.

Grog can be bought commercially under the trade name "brick dust," or it can be made by pulverizing dried raw clay and firing it in an unglazed clay container. Interesting color effects can be gotten by using colored grog in a white clay or a white grog in a colored body. To get

Color, shrinkage, and vitrification are all affected by the firing temperature. When making tests, the heat should be recorded with the other data. The temperature of the kiln is estimated by the use of pyrometric cones which melt at various temperatures. These cones are set into the kiln and watched through peepholes. They measure not the immediate temperature, but the "heat-soak," a time-temperature relationship. The numbering system is from Cone 022, 1085° F to Cone 42, 3659° F. A good temperature for firing most terra cotta sculptures is Cone 06, 1841° F; but any heat ranging from Cone 010 to Cone 3 is satisfactory.

Modeling for Terra Cotta

To further our knowledge of modeling for terra cotta, let us follow a piece step by step from the beginning to the finish (Figures 73 to 88). First, we have mixed a sufficient amount of clay as follows:

> 12 pounds Champion and Challenger ball clay
> 12 pounds Ohio shale
> 2 pounds 40-mesh grog
> 3 pounds 20-mesh grog
> 1 pound red iron oxide
> 4 ounces barium carbonate

This is wedged and covered with clean damp towels to retain its moisture.

With a reasonably clear concept in mind, a modeling board of proper dimensions is selected, and a wooden dowel is pushed into a hole drilled at such an angle that the dowel will correspond to the axis of the upright mass of the design (Figure 73). Quite freely, the clay is built into a kind of core of the eventual form, horizontally and vertically (Figure 74). By continuing this procedure the basic form of the entire three-dimensional design is established as quickly as possible. The arms are quite fragile at this stage and must be handled with care until they dry sufficiently to become sturdy (Figure 75). The major masses are further developed by building bit by bit over the entire

93

77

78

79

80

81

82

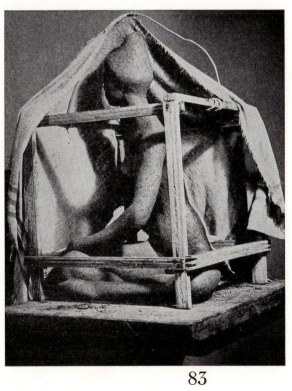

83

84

85

86

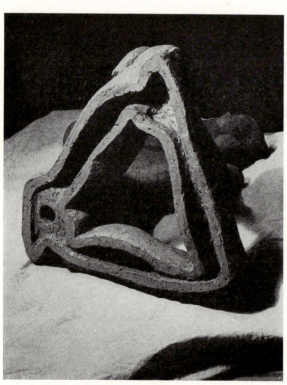

87

88

body; corrections and changes in design are made freely and the form begins to take on its final character (Figures 76-79).

Before the form is finished but after all the major masses are established and there is little likelihood of changes, much of the necessary hollowing out can be done. A good system of doing this is shown in Figures 80 and 81. Cutting incisions in the most strategic areas of the form, a wire-end modeling tool, spoon, or gouge is used to carve out the clay so that a ½-inch wall is left. The entire torso and head are hollowed out but not the arms because they are a little less than one inch thick and will fire without trouble if the heat is raised slowly in the kiln. When the armature is removed, it will leave a ¼-inch hole through the neck. The lower part of the design can be carved out from underneath, but the clay is still rather soft, so this is left for later. When the hollowing of the upper shapes is completed, the clay around the incisions is scratched and brushed with water to soften it. Clay which is only slightly softer than that in the form is kneaded into this softened area and the holes filled. It is important that the clay used in patching is not too soft or there will be more shrinkage in it and a crack will result.

Now that the clay is only ½-inch thick, drying will be quite rapid. To counteract this action, the clay is sprayed or sprinkled periodically with small amounts of water to keep the surface workable (Figure 82). A rack similar to that shown in Figure 83 is constructed, and thoroughly dampened, but not dripping, towels are used to keep the clay properly for several days until work is complete. Actually, the porosity of this particular mixture will cause the clay to pick up moisture, and it will be considerably softer after several hours under the damp towels.

The development of the form continues by applying increasingly smaller bits of clay with the fingers or modeling tools, until the sculpture is completed (Figures 84 and 85). Then, after drying to leather-hard, the clay is lifted straight up from the board with a twisting motion to free the armature and is laid carefully down on a bed of dry towels. Hollowing out from the bottom is completed, and the entire design, except for the arms, is now an even thickness (Figure 86).

Since the design is to be mounted on a wooden base after firing, some method of anchoring must be devised. A small slab of leather-hard clay with a hole in the middle is built into the bottom of the torso, making it possible to use a toggle bolt for fastening on the base. In addition, two hollow areas are made under the knee and foot which, after firing, will be filled with lead and tapped for bolts (Figure 87). These areas are undercut—that is, shaped so that the lead which is poured into them cannot be pulled out when it has solidified.

The clay is allowed to dry out thoroughly and is fired to a temperature of about 1850° F (Cone 06). When cooled, it is removed from the kiln, now a rich red in color, and is mounted on a mahogany base (Figure 88).

Hollow Building: The Coil Method

The problem of supporting large masses of plastic clay in some designs can be solved best by using the coil method of construction. Generally speaking, this is a system of building up hollow shapes by rolling out strips of grogged clay and attaching them edgewise, one above the other. The design progresses slowly and deliberately. The lower portion is finished completely and allowed to dry while the upper parts are being constructed.

This technique is most satisfactory for large designs which are clearly visualized in the beginning. The weight problem is solved in two ways: the masses which are made hollow with walls about ½ inch thick are relatively light; and, since the clay becomes hard before excessive weight is added above it, the structural strength is increased greatly. Unless the design is well established in the mind, though, the technique will tend to control the form completely. In using this method for the first time, a simple design worked out in a sketch should be used. As you become more aware of the nature of the technique, it will only be necessary for you to visualize the form clearly before starting the construction.

The grog clay should be wedged thoroughly, not only to attain an even consistency but to remove as much air as possible from the mixture. To do this, a slight variation in the wedging procedure described in Chapter 4 is used. When the ingredients are combined and the kneaded mass cut on the wedging board wire, one half is thrown firmly against the board and the other thrown with equal force on top of it. This action is repeated a number of times until all large air pockets are eliminated and the section of the mass presents a smooth, unbroken surface when cut on the wire. A large rolling pin can be used to flatten the material into a slab ½ inch in thickness. Strips of the slab can be cut with a knife; these should be about one inch wide and long enough to go completely around the shape. Beveling the ends in opposite directions and allowing them to overlap will help to make a good joint. The edge of the next strip of clay is attached to the top edge of this one by scoring the surface, brushing it with water, and working the clay together with the point of a modeling tool.

During each session of work the modeling and texturing must be completed on that portion of the form, since theoretically, at least, no additional work will be done on that area. In some cases it is possible to rework a dry section by softening it with water, but this should be avoided whenever possible because of the danger of cracking. At the end of each working period the top coil is covered with a damp cloth so that it will not be much harder than the one that is added to it. The other coils are allowed to dry completely.

Hollow Building: Cylinder Construction

Another method of hollow construction is making hollow shapes and joining them together. This technique requires the additional skill of throwing clay shapes on a potter's wheel. Like the coil method it is best for large pieces. An additional form control is introduced by the geometric character of the thrown shapes. In designing for this technique the form should be composed of parts which are basically cylindrical, conical, or spherical in shape. These basic shapes may be cut or modeled slightly but their geometric character should not be destroyed. A sketch, either drawn or three-dimensional, is necessary to establish the sizes of the parts and the manner in which they are to be cut and joined.

Throwing on a potter's wheel, like glazing, is a process that belongs more to the field of ceramics than to sculpture. There are a number of books on pottery making which demonstrate this process in detail.

99

The following is only a general explanation, to give an idea of the steps involved.

Potter's wheels are of two kinds: kick wheels, which are operated by the foot, and power wheels, which have a mechanical source of power. The wheel-head is a revolving disc of steel or aluminum on which the clay is worked into shape. Usually, clay for throwing does not contain coarse grog because of its abrasive character. However, very fine grog can be used and is quite helpful in strengthening the thrown shapes. The clay should be wedged until thoroughly mixed and free of air. The amount needed for a particular shape is estimated and made into a rough ball. This is thrown firmly down as near the center of the disc as possible. Then, with the wheel revolving at a moderate speed, the clay ball is centered. This is done by wetting the hands and the clay, placing the palms on the ball, and keeping the hands rigid by bracing the elbows against the body. Pressure is exerted toward the center of the wheel as the off-center portion of the clay moves against the hands. When the ball is centered the clay is drawn up into a cone two or three times the height of the original ball. Then, exerting pressure on the top of the cone with one hand and keeping the mass centered with the other, you flatten the cone into a short cylindrical shape. The purpose of this step is to condition the clay thoroughly before opening it and drawing it up into a hollow shape. Pressure with the thumbs in the center of the clay will make the initial centered opening. Placing the fingers of one hand and the thumb of the other inside and moving away from the center while slightly squeezing the clay will increase the opening to the desired diameter. At this stage the clay is in the shape of a short hollow cylinder with a thick wall. To draw it up while simultaneously reducing the thickness of the wall, one hand is placed inside and one outside. Equal pressure is applied to the wall by the forefingers as the hands are moved upward. This step is repeated until the wall is about ½ inch thick. By applying more pressure toward the center the shape can be narrowed in diameter. In this case the outer hand presses the wall inward and the inner hand supports the clay. To spread the shape the opposite action is used, but less force is necessary than when reducing the diameter.

Throughout the throwing process, two things are important: the clay should be kept well lubricated with water and the hands kept rigid by bracing the arms against the body. Throwing well is mostly a matter of learning to control the revolving clay through various actions of the hands and practicing these actions until they become almost automatic.

When a shape for a design has been finished, it is cut from the wheel by drawing a wire under it and then lifted by inserting two thin pieces of sheet metal underneath it from opposite sides. It should be set aside to dry to the leather-hard stage before handling. Sometimes it is desirable to bend a shape slightly; this should be done while the clay is still pliable. After all the shapes are thrown and dried, they can be trimmed and fitted together. The joining is done by scoring the surfaces of the joint, wetting them with water or slip, and pressing the parts together. Surface modeling, which should be kept to a minimum, follows the procedure for working over hardened clay surfaces described earlier.

9· Stone Carving

THE ARGUMENT as to which is the superior sculptural method, modeling or carving, is an old one. There is no answer, since obviously they are both techniques for creating formal images, which are either good or bad independently of the technique used. The differences in the two methods are more apparent than real. Both involve the manipulation of mass and space: in the one mass is built up and space is carved, in the other space is modeled while mass is carved. If, as in the recent past, modeling has been abused, this should be blamed on the sculptors' concepts and not on the technique; carving, too, is often abused.

Carving Techniques

Learning to carve teaches us not only another technique for producing sculpture but a new way of conceiving form: the sculpture is precontained within the mass of material, and we must first visualize it and then release it.

There are at least three methods of approach in carving, differing mostly in the beginning and early stages of development: (1) cut off all the obviously excess stone, working generally over the entire mass;

(2) draw outlines of front and profile and cut along these at right angles to the front and side planes; (3) starting from one side of the material, locate the planes that touch the surface and follow them back into the block, releasing the form by cutting the material from around it.

Each of these is a valid method of carving, provided the form that is sought in the material is clearly visualized. However, for teaching purposes, the third technique is preferable to the other two. Looking for the excess is another way of visualizing the form, but it may throw too much emphasis on the material that is cut off at the expense of the remaining sculpture. A beginner, cutting around outlines, may not experience completely the three-dimensionality of the form and may arrive at a sculpture consisting primarily of two silhouettes. Further discussion of this approach is presented in the following chapter on wood carving. The third technique has the advantages of keeping the visualized form foremost in the mind, and of focusing more attention on its existence in three dimensions. It is the process that is described in this chapter.

Stone and Marble

Before we discuss this technique in detail, let us first look at our materials and tools. Stone, the term applied to sedimentary rock formations such as limestone and sandstone, is a brittle, granular mass. Minute organic remains, shells, bones, coral, etc., deposited by water over a period of many thousands of years, make up the substance of limestone. Cementation of the particles of calcium carbonate in this gigantic graveyard turned the particles into a solid mass. Further chemical changes through heat and pressure, in some cases, transformed the granular limestone into crystalline structured marbles. Sandstone is an impure mass of silicon dioxide cemented together by calcium carbonate or ferric oxide.

Above all, stone is real; its hard, heavy massiveness, its cold immobility and formal dignity cause one to feel its presence more strongly, probably, than any other material. It so obviously displaces space and seems to state emphatically that it always was and always will be.

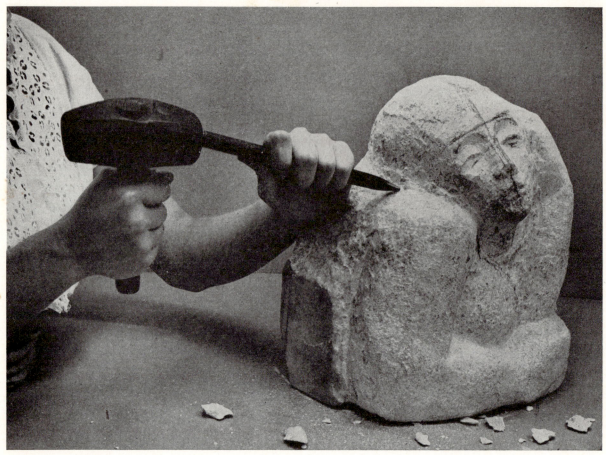

89

There are many varieties of stone and marble, some more suitable for sculpture than others. For beginners, a good grade of limestone, such as the popular Indiana limestone, or inexpensive Georgia marble is best. The limestone is easier to carve but the marble is perhaps a more exciting material, having a more vibrant inner life. Unless one has had some experience with stone, it is wise to ask for specific advice before buying a stone. Most stone yards and monument constructors have professional stone carvers who are usually willing to help.

As with all materials, we must work with stone to realize its nature fully. Words simply cannot take the place of actually shaping a piece of stone.

90

Stone-carving Tools

Stone can be carved by hand or with pneumatic tools. There is little difference in the two methods; when carving with a mallet (Figure 89), you hit fewer and harder blows, while with a pneumatic hammer (Figure 90) the actuating piston held against the chisel makes up for its lesser power by hitting faster. In actual carving time, progress is about the same, though obviously one uses more energy cutting by hand and must work in shorter stretches. Neither is more sensitive than the other; sensitiveness is in the carver, not the tool, and mastery of either method will enable him to impart it to the stone.

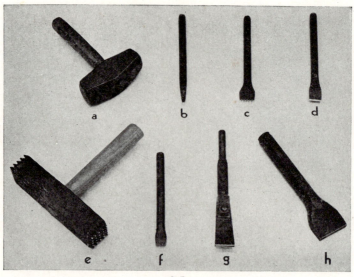

91

The basic hand carving tools shown in Figure 91 are simple, consisting of: the mallet (a), a short handled iron hammer weighing about two pounds; the point (b), for rough carving; the tooth chisel or claw tool (c), for working over the initial rough planes; and the flat chisel (d), for sharpening planes and edges and cleaning up the surface. These are all that is necessary to carve a piece of stone. However, a few special tools will save time and offer more latitude to the work. The bush hammer (e) has heads cut into a series of points which pulverize small projections and even up rough areas when it is pounded against the stone. The frosting tool (f) has an end similar to the bush hammer but with much smaller points. Held at right angles to the nearly finished surface and struck lightly with the mallet it produces a soft texture. The bush chisel (g) is a series of flat blades bolted into a stock. Also a texturing tool, it is used like the frosting tool, but makes a crisper texture. The bull set (h) is used for breaking off large pieces of stone around edges and corners. It is shaped like a flat chisel except that instead of being sharp, the edge is a beveled plane which is held flush against the stone when in use. The tools illustrated are a convenient size for most small carvings. All are available in various sizes.

Pneumatic hammers (Figure 92, a, b, and c) are made with varying sizes of air chambers but all have a ½-inch opening for the tool, so that any of the three hammers can be used with any tool with a ½-inch

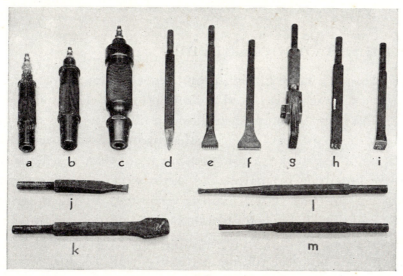

92

shank. The smallest hammer (a) has a ½-inch air chamber, weighs a little over one pound, and its piston moves rapidly even at low pressure. The ¾-inch hammer (b) weighs 1¾ pounds, and hits considerably harder than the smaller one. The largest (c) has a 1-inch air chamber, weighs nearly 4 pounds, and hits relatively slow but hard blows. A source of compressed air and a regulator to control the pressure are necessary to operate the hammers. Most carving is done with the air pressure set between 30 and 40 pounds, but this may be increased and the large hammer used for heavy cutting, or decreased and the small one used for very light carving. Increasing the pressure also speeds up the striking piston.

Pneumatic tools are identical to hand tools except that they all have ½-inch shanks. The point, tooth chisel, and flat chisel (Figure 92, d, e, and f) are used for practically the same purposes as the corresponding hand tools, but the bush chisel (g) and the machine tooth chisel (h) are used in place of the bush hammer. These two are also used along with the frosting tool (i) for surface texturing. The fishtail chisel (j) and the gouge (k) were forged from flat chisels for specific carving problems in wood which are discussed in the following chapter. The drill (l) is used for drilling holes and the cope chisel (m) for cutting and cleaning up small lines and planes. Like the hand tools, all these can be obtained in various sizes.

Planning a Stone Carving

A good plan for a stone carving presupposes the interdependency of a stone idea, a stone design, and a stone of particular kind, size, and shape. Most stone is obtained in six-sided blocks, and we shall assume that this is the shape you have. Further, we will assume the size to be moderate, not less than ½ cubic foot nor more than 2. We may plan for either limestone or marble. A little experimental carving and finishing on one surface will help in planning; among other things, you will find that stone is chipped or broken off, not cut, and beneath the rough surface there is vibrating life. Coarse grained porous limestone, with its spherical cellular structure, will ask for a quality of form quite different from the compact, crystalline, inner glowing marble. A small sketch in clay will help in visualizing the form within the block, but you should be careful not to wear out an idea before beginning the carving.

In transferring the mental image to the stone, a system similar to the following should be used. On newsprint paper draw actual size the outline of each of the six sides of the block, arranging them in proper sequence. In each of these areas, make orthographic drawings of the mental image as seen from that side, fitting the design-idea to the dimensions of the stone so that the outermost projections touch the surfaces of the sides. All this should be done deliberately but with freedom since you want to retain a certain amount of flexibility throughout the carving. The drawings are then transferred to the block of stone. The original drawings are kept because from time to time it will be necessary to refer to them or to redraw them on the stone.

Carving Procedure

The question of which side to begin carving from must be answered individually, but generally it should be the side containing the most complex organization of form, which in some cases is the top. Having determined this, by consulting the adjacent drawings, find the part of the form which touches that surface. Start carving at this junction, using the point tool to chip stone from around the planes as they

93

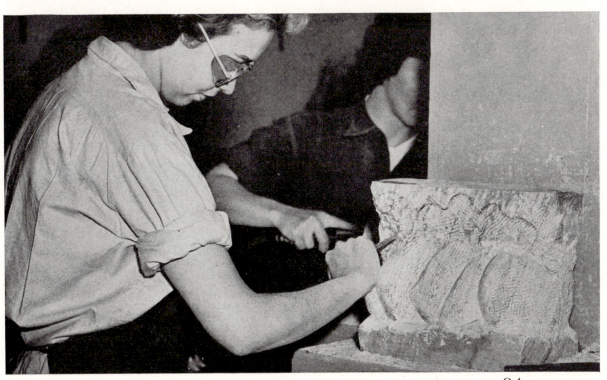

94

move back in the block. Make use of the drawings to determine directions and clean up the surfaces with a tooth chisel to clarify the planes. In a few minutes, you will have released part of the form, and visualization within the block will become clearer (Figure 93).

The carving progresses by removing a layer approximately one inch thick across the entire side, releasing roughly but clearly whatever part of the form exists in that layer. Carve with the point, changing to the tooth chisel only periodically to straighten up the planes. Be sure to consult the drawings in all three dimensions. For instance, in Figure 93 the highest point on the side that is being carved seems to come right on the edge of that side and the top, but a glance at the drawing on the end shows that it actually is situated about half way back in the block. Furthermore, the end drawing shows the degree of vertical curvature of the planes being carved while the top drawing indicates the horizontal extremities.

Corners and edges of the stone are retained until their presence hampers the progress of releasing the sculpture. The formality of the block serves as spatial reference until the form of the sculpture is definite enough for this purpose. In other words, you begin carving on the planes of the sculpture and establish them in space as the planes of the block disappear; there is never a time when the mass of stone is disorganized and chaotic (Figure 94).

Some allowance should be made for minor changes and surfacing; ⅛ inch or even ¼ inch may be necessary in places. However, the progress of the carving is such that the form is definitely established as it is released from the block (Figures 95 and 96). Throughout the procedure you must visualize, and this becomes easier as more and more of the sculpture emerges from the block. From the beginning, the line drawings give way to the actual three-dimensional shape that is established, and toward the end there is little or no consideration of the original drawings.

When all the major planes of the sculpture have been established the original block will have disappeared except for its virtual planes, which almost invariably remain in a good carving. The machine tooth chisel and the frosting tool may be used to advantage in unifying the form (Figure 97). Minor adjustments of planes, accents, and textures

95

96

97

may involve the use of various tools, such as the tooth chisel, flat chisel, frosting tool, and bush chisel.

As explained above, the value of this technique is primarily as an aid in visualization in the third dimension, but it also assures a good balance of control between the mind of the sculptor and the dictates of the stone. Too often, in carving by other methods, students either follow the line of least resistance and allow the stone to take complete charge of the situation, or in their determination to subdue the stone, they give it no voice at all.

Once a form is seen clearly in a block of stone, and after you have gained some confidence in your ability to carve, ceremonious technique may be laid aside, and the most direct methods used. There is, for instance, no reason for limiting the initial cutting to a depth of one inch if the form is clear in your mind.

The technique used for carving the pink Georgia marble *Mother and Child* (Figures 98-106) is similar to the one described above except that there was less emphasis on individual planes in the early development. The form was released as a massive unit, and minor planes were carved in later stages.

Incidentally, the break in the bottom corner of the marble in Figure 98 was in the block originally and the form had to be planned so as to compensate for it. Notice how it affected the design. Sculptors find this a frequent occurrence, especially those who start with irregular shapes. If it seems unusual that an accidental break should play a part in a formal design, remember that the artist's job is making arbitrariness into meaningful order. Some sculptors find it easier to visualize in irregularly shaped stones and prefer to carve from boulders and other natural stone shapes.

The action of the point on the marble shows clearly in Figures 98 and 99. It is a very flexible tool and should be used as much as possible in the initial carving. Overuse of the tooth chisel should be avoided since, being flat, it tends to control the character of the form, and its overuse often results in a misleading, premature finish. The big advantage of the claw tool is that it cuts small grooves for itself which guide it evenly over the surface and prevent digging in and lateral slipping. After masses are established with the point, the tooth chisel is used conservatively to clarify the planes (Figures 100 and 101).

98

99

100

101

102 103

104 105

106 a

b

c

d

e

f

The progress of the carving in Figures 102-105 is obvious: the entire mass released from the block (Figure 102); clarification of the form (Figure 103); and the smoothing of the child's body, which was done with a flat chisel (Figures 104 and 105). The polishing of the child's body and parts of the mother's hands and feet (Figure 106) was done by filing, then by rubbing the marble first with wet waterproof sandpaper (No. 400 grit) and finally with a paste made of putty powder and water. The other textures were obtained by using the flat chisel, frosting tool, and bush chisel.

The bird form in Figure 107 was made in a similar manner. It, also, was carved in pink Georgia marble. The bill and feet were polished and a frosting tool was used on the body, not to imitate feathers but to abstract their quality of softness. The limestone animal in Figure 108 is a good example of stone-controlled form. Notice how the limestone quality in it differs from the marble quality of the abstraction in Figure 97.

107   108

10· Wood Carving

USING the previous discussion (Chapter 6) as a basis, we will investigate further the character of wood and methods of carving it, exploring more of its possibilities as a sculptural medium.

First, it may be wise to say a few words about the visual appeal of material and the danger of falling completely under its spell. During the development of a sculpture, we meet a number of paths tangent to the course of the original sculptural idea. Overemphasis on literal meaning at the expense of visual expression, and weak attempts at reproducing nature have been discussed earlier. Of these tangent paths, probably none is more beguiling than the esthetic appeal of the material. This often exciting road can be easily mistaken for our true direction, but, as in the case of all tangents, if we follow it far enough, we will arrive at a point quite different from our original goal. Just as a sculpture often suffers from a lack of consideration of materials, so it may become weak through excessive emphasis on the material aspect. We must not be lured by the esthetic appeal of a surface or a particular effect to forget our purpose, the prime mover and over-all control of our sculpture.

A sculptural idea presumes a certain amount of visual expression from the material itself, but when this expression speaks only of the material, it is not sculptural. In other words, a sculptor, in harmonious cooperation with his material, makes use of its visual characteristics for his own purposes. When he allows himself to become simply the agent of the material, he is not being a sculptor. Similarly, one whose primary purpose is lost in a technique becomes only a technician.

Wood Grain

One of the most intriguing aspects of wood and the one most apt to lead the sculptor astray is wood grain. Though we should not and cannot ignore the grain, we must carve with most of our attention focused on three-dimensional shapes, lest the grain become quite dictatorial. If we retain the control of the shapes, the grain will, in most cases, enhance the form by emphasizing directions and by creating unifying rhythms over the design.

Understanding in a general way the effects of the concentric conical growth rings on particular kinds of form will help in anticipating the final result, and will enable us to plan accordingly. Some design-ideas may be accentuated by the rhythmical flow of the grain; in others, the grain may interfere with the visual character of the form, and wood with less obvious grain must be used. In the planning stage, we should be interested only in the general pattern of the grain, remembering that the shapes will change in the process of carving. Anticipating the exact markings of the final surface, if such were possible, would be little more than a problem in geometry, and would restrict the transformation of the idea into wood form.

The two pieces of yellow pine in Figure 109 with the strong tonal contrast of spring and summer growth, show clearly the effects of various kinds of cutting on the structure of the annual rings. The front cross-sectional plane of the block, called end grain, is a graphic, year-by-year account of the life of the tree. (The dark, ray-like shapes, branching out from the center, are deposits of resin and not a part of the growth pattern.) The top and side show the concentric conical structure of the tree trunk. Notice that where the cut is nearly tangent

109

to these cones, the grain pattern becomes very broad and, as the cut approaches a right angle to the ring, the stripes become progressively smaller. The degree of consistency in the cones and the evenness of the cut determine the regularity of the pattern. The curved cutting of the form on the right shows the three-dimensional extension of this principle of tangential and radial cutting. The flat patterns of the two-dimensional planes of the block are transformed into three-dimensional rhythms as the cutting becomes more curved. The flow of the grain pattern follows closely the movement of the planes, but it resists complete accord to the same extent that the growing tree resisted complete geometrization.

The grain of yellow pine is more obvious than that of most woods. Some varieties of mahogany have such a subtle grain that it is imperceptible unless highly polished. Most fruit- and nut-bearing trees, such as cherry, apple, and walnut, have a grain and texture well suited to carving. Such tropical woods as teakwood, rosewood, ebony, and lignum vitae are excellent for sculpture, though the latter two are quite hard.

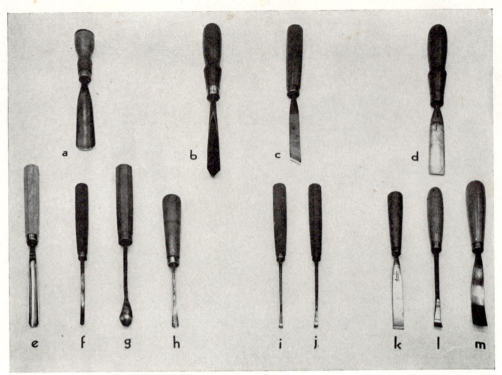

110

Wood-carving Tools

Wood carving, like stone carving, demands only a few simply shaped, basic tools, each designed to meet a specific need in the carving process. These tools, shown in Figure 110, are as follows: (a) The gouge is a curved edged tool for rapid, rough cutting; the shape helps to guide it evenly through the wood. (b) The parting tool is V shaped and is used for cutting sharp lines and cleaning up angular junctions of planes. (c) The skew chisel is flat, with its edge at an angle to the axis of the blade; it is used in corners and in cutting which requires a point. (d) The flat chisel is used for making sharp, flat cuts and smoothing planes.

Variations in size, curvature, and shape of the blade in these basic tools result in the variety shown in the lower row in Figure 110. The U gouge (e), bent gouge (f), spoon gouge (g) and fishtail gouge (h) solve practically all problems of cutting requiring a curved edge. The left and right bent skew chisels (i and j) are seldom used but when one is needed for getting into a corner, no other tool will do. The edge

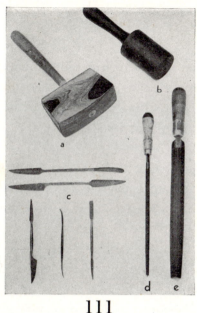

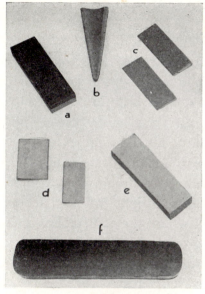

111   112

of the flat chisel (k) is beveled on both sides; the short bent chisel (l) and the long bent chisel (m) are used where a particular angle is required in cutting.

The two types of mallets (a and b in Figure 111) vary in weight from one to three pounds; the choice of which to use is personal. The rifflers (c) are carefully made files of varying sizes and shapes. They are used for texturing and for removing small projections of wood which, for some reason, cannot be cut off with a cutting tool. The round rasp (d) is used for smoothing in small openings. The half-round rasp (e) is used mostly for smoothing end grain.

The sharpening stones shown in Figure 112 are of two kinds, silicon carbide or aluminum oxide synthetic stones and the naturally occurring Arkansas stones. The combination stone (a) is made of aluminum oxide heated to the point of vitrification. It has a coarse side for fast grinding and a fine side for smoothing an edge. Most of the sharpening is done on this stone. The gouge slip stone (b) is helpful in finishing the curved edges of gouges. The round edge slip stones (c) are also used for finishing the edges of gouges. The Arkansas slip stones (d) and Arkansas bench stone (e) are fine, almost glassy, finishing stones used for obtaining a very sharp edge. The leather covered block (f) is used only when a razor-sharp edge is needed.

121

The Sharpening Process

In order to take and hold a keen edge, wood-carving tools must be made of a high-grade steel which is tempered through heat treatment. This temper is an important factor in the quality of the tool; while it makes the steel quite brittle, the concomitant hardness is necessary for retaining a sharp edge.

For the sake of clarity let us divide the sharpening process into two phases: (1) shaping, which includes grinding the edge to its proper curve or straight line and forming of the concave or hollow-ground bevel where the tool tapers to its edge, and (2) sharpening, which is the process of grinding the edge to its proper thinness and then reducing the more or less jagged, saw-like projections of the edge to a more even and smoother line.

The shaping is done on a grind wheel, either hand or power driven. The edge is shaped by holding the axis of the blade at a right angle to the moving wheel. In the case of the U gouges, it is wise to sweep back the ends of the curve so that when driven or pushed into wood there is less strain on the metal. However, if this is overdone, the projecting part of the curve will be weakened.

A hollow-ground bevel serves two purposes: the tapering end of the tool enters wood with less force, and the hollow surface makes the finishing and resharpening easier, as we shall see later. We hollow grind the bevel by holding the back of the tool against the circumference of the grind wheel at an angle of from 30° to 45° below the horizontal (Figure 113). Increasing the angle makes a broader bevel and reducing it makes the bevel narrower. For most carving the width should be about ½ inch; for cutting very hard wood it should be ¼ inch or slightly less.

The process of hollow grinding is the same for chisels and gouges except for the movement of the tool in relation to the wheel; flat bevels are moved laterally across the turning wheel but curved bevels must be rotated so that the grinding is even across the entire bevel. The tool must be held at a constant angle and ground slowly, so as not to let enough friction heat build up to burn the temper from the metal. The tool should be dipped in water or oil periodically to help keep it cool; thin metal heats quickly, and once it becomes hot enough to

113   114

darken, the temper is lost in that spot. Because of the circular shape of the wheel, the first grinding will occur halfway between the edge and the opposite extremity or heel of the bevel. As the grinding continues, the bevel becomes deeper in the middle and curves out to the edge and heel. Actually, there should be little, if any, grinding on the edge itself. Unless the edge is thick and uneven, that part is left for the oilstones; the shaping ends when the curve of the bevel reaches the edge and heel. If it is necessary to grind on the thickness of the edge with a power grinder, this should be done before the bevel is ground. The back of the edge is held lightly against the flat side of the wheel until the edge line is thin and even. It is good practice to check the thickness of this line often to see where additional grinding is needed; the metal is removed rapidly, and overgrinding will result in an unevenly shaped edge.

123

Finishing the Edge

With our tool properly shaped and hollow ground, finishing the edge is easy. Unless the end of the tool is broken, it will not need reshaping for a long time. The first step in finishing the edge of a gouge on the coarse side of the combination stone is shown in Figure 114. A small amount of oil is used to float the ground-off metal particles and prevent filling in between the crystals of the stone, which would cause it to lose its "bite."

Holding the bevel against the stone, we can see the advantage of hollow grinding; only the edge and heel touch the stone, which means that there is little metal to grind off. Starting at the center of the edge, with both the edge and heel pressed firmly against the stone, we move the gouge forward with a twisting motion, so that half the length of the bevel is ground in one stroke. Then, we retract and start again from the center, and the tool is twisted in the opposite direction to grind the other half. After this is repeated a few times the edge line should be inspected to see that the grinding is even. When the white line disappears, the edge is of proper thinness for this stage, but if looked at with a magnifying glass, its unevenness can be seen. The small projections of metal causing this jaggedness are called the "burr" or "wire edge." Some of this can be removed by turning the stone over and continuing the grinding on the fine side, but the most efficient method is to use the India slip stone as shown in Figure 115. For this process, hold the tool upright and rub the flat side of the stone downward against the edge, moving evenly around the curve. Then, turning the tool around, use the round edge of the stone in a similar manner on the inside of the curve, moving parallel to the axis of the blade to prevent making a bevel on the inside. The burr can be felt with the fingers and should be removed entirely before cutting with the tool; if it is broken off by forcing the edge into wood, dull spots will result.

Once this burr is removed the tool is sharp enough for most carving. However, just as the coarse stones create a wire edge, the finer stones used for grinding it off make another smaller burr. If an exceptionally sharp edge is needed, as in texturing and cutting across the grain, the tool can be given additional sharpening with the Arkansas stones. The manner of using these stones is identical to that of

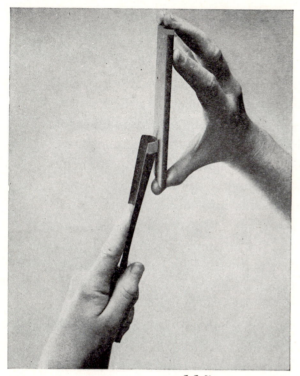
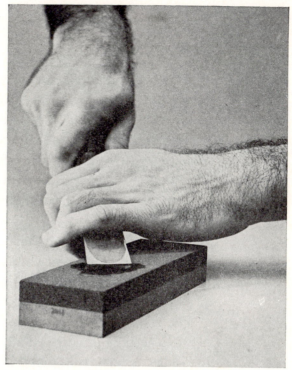

115   116

the corresponding India stones. The leather-covered block may be used to remove any burr left by the Arkansas stones, and to align the minute teeth of the edge. The tool should be pulled backward in a straight line over the leather block, the opposite of the movement used on the stones.

The chisels are considerably easier to bring to a keen edge than the gouges, for we do not have to contend with a curved surface. The bevel of the chisel is held evenly against the stone and pushed forward (Figure 116). If the tool is beveled on both sides, the grinding is alternated, one stroke on one side and one on the other, using even pressure against the stone. The burr is removed by the same movement on the fine side of the India combination stone and the Arkansas bench stone.

While we are carving, the edge of the tool should be inspected frequently. The reappearance of the white line will indicate dullness. Unless the edge is broken or gets very dull, the tool can be kept sharp with occasional use of the India and Arkansas slips.

125

Power Tools

Those tools operated partially by a constant mechanical source of power but requiring a certain amount of guidance are called power tools. Since they are so widely used commercially, an abundance of printed descriptions and instructions is available at large hardware stores, and there is no need of repeating that information here. We will be concerned primarily with the general application of power tools to shaping wood, leaving more specific information to individual research.

Some mention has been made of the use of the jigsaw and drill press in Chapter 6. Other machines which may be helpful to the sculptor are the bench saw, bandsaw, the abrasive machine or sander, the lathe, and the sand blast.

The reluctance of the sculptor to use mechanical tools can be justified to a certain extent. Hand tools are more flexible, depending upon the sculptor for force as well as guidance, and result in a freer kind of cutting. The power necessary for each stroke can be anticipated, and the sculptor can feel his way into the material. Machines, on the other hand, are individualistic, each insisting on imparting its particular character to the material.

Looking more closely at the situation, however, we find that there is less difference in the two categories of tools than first consideration indicates. Hand tools are not completely flexible, especially in the hands of a beginner; the gouge will simply make grooves when pushed into a piece of wood, and only through understanding of the possibilities and limitations of the tool can one find its flexibility. If this kind of understanding is developed of machines, they too become more flexible. Anyone who watches an experienced foundry pattern-maker at work will realize that power tools are much more than time- and labor-saving devices, and that with the proper approach one can find much freedom in the use of machines. What is most important is first to learn the character of the machine, and then to make use of its possibilities when they are applicable to our needs, not asking it to perform outside this realm of possibilities. Actually, this is the same requirement hand tools demand.

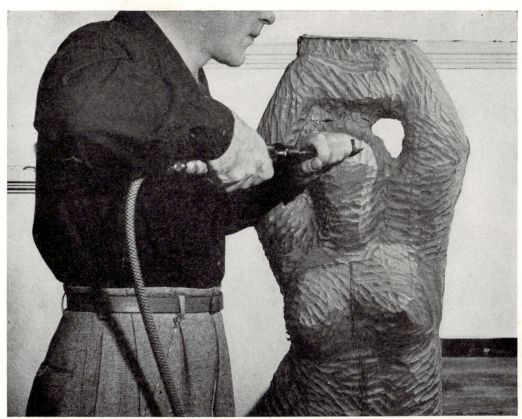

117

The Use of Pneumatic Tools for Wood Carving

In the sense described above, the pneumatic tool cannot be called a machine or power tool. As was pointed out in the preceding chapter on stone carving, the control of the force is as sensitive as the control over our own muscles. At times it is even more flexible than hand tools, since the action of its use is closer to that of pushing a tool into the material than of driving it in with a mallet.

As in the case of machines, the application of the pneumatic hammer to wood carving is limited; well-sharpened hand tools are adequate for most cutting. The most important use of the pneumatic hammer is in carving on the hard end grain. Here it has two advantages over

118

regular wood tools: the light but fast blows of the hammer enable one to cut without tearing the wood; and, as softer steel is used for the blade, there is less danger of breaking the tool. No wood-carving tools are available for use in pneumatic hammers, but these can be forged from ordinary stone tools, and shaped and tempered for cutting wood.

Besides allowing much more freedom in the carving of end grain, the pneumatic tools make easier the carving of woods with an uneven hardness of grain, such as yellow pine with its soft spring and hard summer growth. The problem of controlling the depth of the cut and the jumping of the tool is less difficult than with hand tools. Considerable time and labor can be saved also on large carvings (Figures 117 and 118).

The Band-saw Technique

A procedure for carving that is particularly adaptable to wood, and one that will introduce the use of a number of tools as well as presenting an interesting aspect of three-dimensional design, is shown in Figures 119-124.

After choosing a block of wood, study it from various angles considering two questions: "Is the shape expressive of wood?" and "Is the form spatially expressive?" The answer to the first is negative; there is no relationship between the block and wood as a substance. The second question may be answered yes, when three of the six planes are seen simultaneously, but no, when only two planes or one plane can be seen.

Our problem, then, becomes this: how can the block be changed to a more integrated spatial design while also becoming more wood-like in character? All our knowledge of the principles of design and wood, and our feeling for order and the material, should be used in answering the question. Perhaps a subject such as a leaf-shape may act as a catalyst in crystallizing the answer, or we may find a solution through planning the unification of the planes resulting from two silhouettes. In the latter case, two shapes, in harmony with the wood but independent except for height, are planned as front and profile. This will not give us a three-dimensional design, but it will establish a point of departure from which we can visualize within the block. Orthographic working drawings and freehand sketches are very helpful in developing the form idea.

Having the general three-dimensional shape clearly established in the mind, draw the outlines of two adjacent views on the corresponding sides of the block as shown in Figure 119. Notice the independency of the two views; while the shapes here are similar, they need not be, though in that case the problem of unification will be harder to solve.

Next cut the outlines at right angles to each of these sides on a band saw (Figure 120), removing part of the excess wood. The resulting shape (Figure 121) will be more or less startling, depending on how clearly you visualized this stage of development. With the general shape-idea established in the wood, attention may be focused more

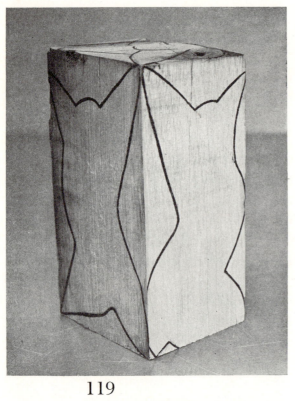

119

120

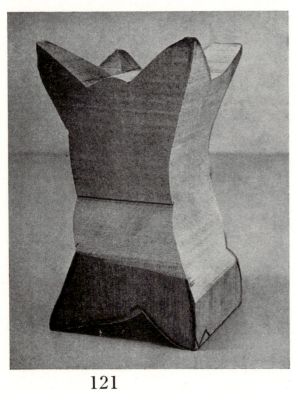

121

122

sharply on the progression of the planes in space. The degree to which this has been planned along with the shape-idea will determine the success and ease of attaining unity in the final design. Some deviation from plans is inevitable, however, and much of the quality of the design hinges on how carefully you handle the next phase of the carving.

Studying the design, you find that, in spite of the similarity of silhouettes, the planes are not knitted together but simply juxtaposed; the views neither anticipate each other nor work together to make a unified image in the mind. Beginning with the larger changes in these plane relationships, draw the boundaries of the new interlocking planes, indicating generally where wood is to be removed.

The block is held firmly in a vise, and the carving started with a sharp gouge (Figure 122). The tool should be pushed into the wood whenever possible, and the mallet reserved for hard cutting such as removing large quantities of wood or cutting directly across the end grain. Three different directions of cutting are possible: with the grain and across the grain (which have been described earlier) and diagonally with the grain and slightly across it. Each of these will be found advantageous at times. Cutting with the grain results in a smooth cut but one that is difficult to control; cutting across the grain tears the wood unless the tool is very sharp, but the amount of wood taken off can be gauged accurately; diagonal cutting has some of the advantages of both. With a little experience, a twisting motion of the pushing hand enables the tool to enter and leave the wood at will. Both hands should be kept back of the cutting edge and in contact with the tool, one pushing and one guiding the blade, braking its forward movement when it leaves the wood.

Unlike stone carving, wood carving is a process of cutting; the fibers must be severed, vertically or horizontally, in order to control the amount taken off. When you wish to remove large quantities of material, the wood can be splintered along the grain, but usually this is a bad practice since it results in an uncontrolled surface and you seldom are certain where the break will occur.

Establishing some of the major planes of your design will help in visualizing smaller relationships. In Figure 123, the general character

123

124

125

of the final form is beginning to show. The planes are cut freely, allowing some extra material for smoothing. Lines are not emphasized during this stage, but the planes are arranged so that where sharpness of line is needed, the final junction of the planes will be sharp. Particular attention should be paid to the knitting together of three-dimensional movements and to the relationship of shapes of planes to each other and to the total shape, so that the form becomes one unified and visually continuous thing, without independent views or parts.

The matter of handling the surface depends largely on the character of the form. In some cases the crisp tool marks may be retained to give the form a "chopped-out" texture; in others, various degrees of smoothness can be obtained by using the flat chisel, rasp, and sandpaper in that order (Figure 124). On flat planes, a perfectly flat chisel with a square edge will leave a track caused by the corners digging into the wood. To overcome this, these corners should be rounded slightly or a very shallow, almost flat gouge may be used. There is no such problem on curved planes. Sanding can often follow the cutting with a flat chisel, and the rasps can be left for areas impossible to smooth otherwise, such as hollows and end grain.

The three forms in Figure 125 are other solutions to the same problem we have covered. All started with mahogany blocks of similar dimensions, and each found an answer through a particular system of organization which, being in harmony with the material, resulted in an integrated wood design.

The Emerging-form Technique

The method of stone carving described in Chapter 9 is equally applicable to wood carving. We will not take time to go through the entire process again, but will cover only the special problems relating to wood not brought out in the preceding technique.

If you use a large block of wood and do not make the initial cuts with the band saw, you must make more use of the mallet with the concomitant danger of breaking tools. Several general rules kept in mind will help prevent tool breakage and make carving with a mallet simpler.

126

127

128

1. Never drive the tool against the grain.

2. Do not try to make large cuts with a small tool.

3. Be sure the chip of wood rises and loosens the tool after each stroke; if not, pull the tool out and cut the chip off from the opposite direction.

4. Do not try to pry wood loose by using the tool as a lever.

5. Be exceptionally careful when cutting on end grain or knots.

To begin cutting on the flat side of a block, drive the gouge into the wood about ½ inch, holding the tool at a 45° angle. Then, leveling off and holding just sufficient pressure on the handle to retain this depth, drive the gouge with the grain to within an inch of the length of the desired cut. Remove the tool and cut back in the opposite direction to release the chip (Figure 126).

Tools can be controlled much easier when pushed by hand than when driven with a mallet and whenever possible use of the mallet should be avoided. If the gouge is kept sharp and if the grain of the wood is understood, carving can be quite free and rapid. Cutting across the grain is often the most effective way of removing wood and establishing planes as is shown in the partially emerged form in Figure 127. Only broad planes and movements are established in this early stage of carving. Extra wood must be left for more careful shaping and surfacing.

As the form develops, gouges of smaller sizes and various shapes may be needed to apply the necessary force and still cut in the proper direction. The long bent gouge is an excellent tool for getting into enclosed areas, and often the spoon gouge is the only tool that can reach depressed areas. Besides being useful for shaving off the ridges left by the gouge, flat chisels can be used for making short, crisp cuts which lend a vigor to the surface. Smoothing, rasping, or sanding should be done only after careful consideration of its desirability. In many cases, the gouge or chisel strokes accentuate shapes and contours, and much of the life and vigor of expression can be lost through overworking the material.

If left alone, the surface of a piece of wood will turn to its own distinctive color in a short time, darkening as air and light react upon the chemical substances on the surface. A thin coat of linseed oil will

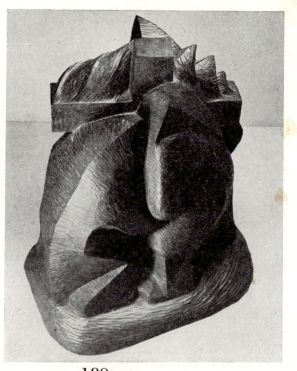

129

130

131

132

darken wood immediately, but in time it causes the surface to become darker than it normally would, and gives an oily feel to the wood. A good grade of paste floor wax is better, since it stains the wood less and has the added advantage of preventing dirt from entering the pores of the wood. A thinly sprayed coat of lacquer serves the same purpose, though if it is applied heavily the surface will have an objectionable shine.

If wood is polychromed, it must be done with considerable planning and experimentation. First, the form must warrant the use of color, and, second, you must be careful not to break the spatial unity or destroy the quality of the material. Restraint should be used in both selecting and applying colors, at least until you have confidence in handling them; rather than being painted, the wood should be lightly stained so as to retain the wood texture. A good technique is to mix oil colors or dry pigments with very thin varnish and turpentine. This mixture should be applied freely with a brush, and wiped immediately with a cloth dampened with turpentine. Experimental applications on a piece of scrap wood will help in finding the right colors and tones. It is wise to build up the color effect by adding several light coats, since excessive pigment is hard to remove, especially from end grain.

The woodcarvings shown in Figures 129-132 are examples of various ways of handling wood form and texture. The heavy, oppressive, block-like shapes in Figure 129 are accentuated by the tool marks. The form was carved almost entirely with gouges from a large block of mahogany. The teakwood torso in Figure 130 was polished to bring out the subtle rhythms of the grain. The corpulent man at the desk (Figure 131) was carved from a mahogany flitch-end, the irregular end of the log from which veneer is sliced. The piece was carved so that one of its sides is the bottom and the grain runs horizontally. Slight polychromy was used along with texture to emphasize some planes and shapes. In Figure 132, the teakwood grain accentuates the rhythms of the plane organization. The wood was worked over with a rasp and sandpaper after carving, but great care was taken to prevent the form from getting soft, a characteristic of most sanded surfaces.

137

11· Relief Sculpture

EARLIER, when we discussed the nature of three-dimensional form, we said there were two categories, space-displacing and space-enclosing. Perhaps we should include a third—illusory or relief form, mass and space that, when seen from the right position and under proper lighting, seem to have more depth than is actually there.

The term *relief* is applied to many kinds of sculpture, ranging from that in which the form is indicated by incised lines to "sculpture in the round" which is attached to a wall or a similar background plane. The amount of emphasis placed on the illusion of depth varies greatly in relief sculptures. For instance, the illusion of distance in Egyptian and Assyrian reliefs is negligible compared to that in Lorenzo Ghiberti's "Gates of Paradise." Often we find sculptures in the round with parts done in relief; in other cases, free-standing forms may be so handled that the effect depends to some extent on an illusion of depth. In the following discussion we will not try to cover all the various kinds of relief form; we will consider primarily one of the basic problems of relief sculpture—that of creating the illusion of depth. We will be particularly interested in the part played by patterns of light and shade in producing this effect.

138

Light and Visual Perception

We do not see surfaces, we see only light; and the manner in which light is reflected or interrupted by planes constitutes the physical stimulus for our visual perception. We distinguish a sphere from a disk by the modulation of the light over its curved surface. This modulation is so constant in pattern that even though the contrast of light and shade is at times small, we seldom mistake the two. Relief form is made by reducing or foreshortening the depth dimension and simulating the normal light patterns to some degree.

This simulation can vary from high relief, where the light pattern approaches that of the actual three-dimensional form under the same lighting conditions, to incised lines, in which simply the outlines are contrasted with those of the planes seemingly behind them, through light and dark. In low relief, much use is made of overlapping planes as an indication of space; the beveling back of a plane as it meets the outline of a plane in front of it simulates a more normal pattern of light against dark than the incised-line technique. The degree to which the depth is reduced determines the amount of exaggeration in the illumination of planes.

Relief Form and Painting

The dependency of relief form, especially low relief, on drawing is obvious; much of the shaping of form and illusion of space is indicated by the two-dimensional interplay of lines. Like drawings and paintings, the conception of a relief presupposes its existence on a wall and consideration for two-dimensional organization and figure-ground relationships. For these reasons, relief form is often said to belong to the field of drawing and painting rather than to sculpture. But since the making of a relief involves the materials, tools, and techniques of the sculptor and is, at least partially, expression in the third dimension, we have to consider it as sculpture, granting its similarities to painting.

Conceptually, there is this difference between a relief and a painting: the painter places his lights and shadows permanently, creating his own light effect which rarely, if ever, coincides with the lighting of other objects surrounding the painting. This imparts a character of "another worldness" to the images; they exist independently in a setting confined to the boundaries of the frame. Relief sculpture, having a light source in common with other objects in its environment, is not independent of its surroundings, but the planes within the relief are so manipulated as to transform the character of the light effect into another kind of "other worldness." For instance, a sphere in relatively flat relief placed beside an actual sphere will be illuminated by the same light source. Unlike the shape which we see in a painting of a sphere, the relief sphere will exist in the same environment as the actual sphere. If the pattern of light reflected from the relief form has been made to correspond generally to that of the actual sphere, there is an illusion of roundness. However, the relief cannot reflect the exact pattern of light as the three-dimensional sphere; thus if we accept the illusion of roundness in the relief then we necessarily see a difference in the quality of light reflected from the two forms. The degree of difference we seem to see in the light quality is determined by the amount of depth illusion; or conversely, the degree of illusion of three-dimensionality in the relief is determined by the amount of difference in light quality we accept. In other words, if a relief form looks "in the round" to us, it will seem to be under a somewhat different light than the three-dimensional objects around it which are illuminated by the same light source.

The readiness with which our minds accept this kind of visual illusion can be observed in looking at concave shapes such as the plaster molds in a sculpture studio. Very often the hollow negative form will seem to protrude outward. In photographing a mold it is quite difficult to arrange the lighting and the position of the form in such a way as to prevent concave shapes from appearing convex. The phenomenon in this situation is very similar to that of which we have been speaking. The light pattern on the concave planes inside the mold is the same as the one that would exist on the convex cast of this mold with the light source from the opposite direction. The mind seems to prefer to see convex rather than concave shapes, even to the

140

extent of accepting a light source for the illusioned form which is the opposite of that illuminating the surrounding objects. This illusion is more persistent in a photograph because there it is easier for the mind to reconcile the conflicting light conditions.

Illusion and Relief Form

Illusion of depth is no more the criterion of relief sculpture than it is the criterion of painting. This is simply one of relief sculpture's means of visual expression, and the amount of emphasis placed on the optical illusion depends upon what we wish to express. From the discussion above, it follows that as the illusion of depth is increased, the tendency of a relief form to separate from its environment increases. And since one of the major problems of visual design is the adapting of forms to their surroundings, restraint should be used in creating illusions of the third dimension. For instance, in architectural sculpture, such as a relief carving on a building, it often may be preferable to retain the unity of the wall surface by keeping the illusion of depth to a minimum. Incised line designs do less to break the consistency of the light emanating from the wall plane than a relief with the illusion of great depth. However, the architectural unity of a wall is not necessarily lost through illusory form in relief, provided the illusion of depth is subordinated to the wall plane and the form is strongly related to the architecture. A well-handled architectural relief decoration enhances the unity of a wall, emphasizing its structure and actualness, as well as relieving the monotony of a large, unbroken expanse of reflected light.

Unity of Planes in Relief

The strongest unifying factor in a relief is its frontal plane which is sometimes called the picture plane; all planes in the form should be subordinated to this plane and closely related to it. Shapes within the design should be selected and arranged so that their most descriptive views are relatively flat planes parallel to the frontal plane. No more than secondary importance should be given to receding planes. Distance is best handled by grouping planes into distinct levels or layers of depth: foreground, middleground, and background, or simply foreground and background. Within each layer there should be a consistency of depth compression; we should allow approximately the same projection for shapes of equal depth.

Reliefs which are primarily linear in character, such as incised lines and very low reliefs, should not be freed of the control of the frontal plane even though the actual planes upon which they are drawn are parallel to this picture plane. The misuse of perspective—that is, the use of perspective without regard to the two-dimensional control of the picture plane—can destroy the unity. In other words, in relief sculpture we should design with the perceptual illusion as well as with the actual planes of the relief. High-relief form depends heavily on virtual planes and lines for its unity with the frontal plane. In some cases, the unifying distance-levels mentioned above may be indicated by illusory virtual planes where there is no actual difference of projection.

Light Source and Relief

In planning a relief, the sculptor must be constantly aware of his dependency upon the light under which the design will be seen. As pointed out, the problem of creating relief form is the problem of manipulating planes so as to exaggerate the normal reflections of light. If a form is made under one set of light conditions and seen under another, the effect may be startling. The two illustrations, Figures 133 and 134, show the results of photographing the same plaster relief under a simple variation in the light source. In Figure 133 the light source was directly in front of the form; in Figure 134 it was shifted to the edge of the relief. A more complex form and greater variations in the intensity and position of the light source would produce stronger differences of effect. A form made under an overhead light and later seen with a light from underneath is almost always totally changed.

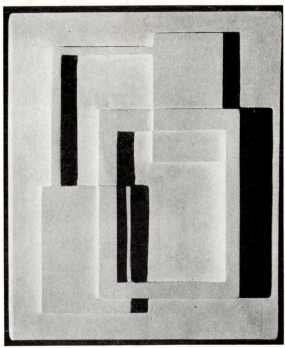

133   134

Techniques of Making Reliefs

Reliefs can be made with any of the techniques and materials used in sculpture. High relief in clay, either for terra cotta or casting, follows the same principles of modeling as form in the round; however, in low relief, where subtle variations in planes are of great importance, considerable carving and scraping may be necessary. Allowance should be made for increased intensity of light reflection when a relief built in clay is to be cast in plaster; a good method to use at times is to build the form roughly in clay, cast it in plaster, and then complete the modeling and carving in the plaster. Low reliefs can sometimes be handled easier by carving on the plaster mold before casting it, remembering that the form will be reversed in the final cast.

Materials such as boards, sheet metal, plastic, and thin reinforced plaster slabs are particularly adaptable to constructions in relief. Much use can be made of power tools in shaping and finishing the various parts of the design before putting them together.

143

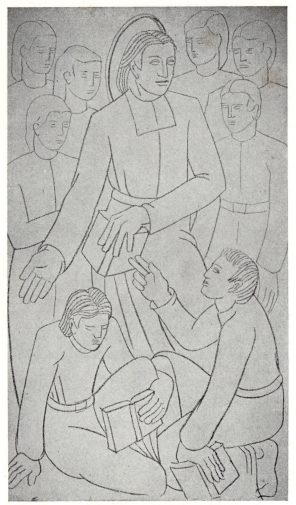

135

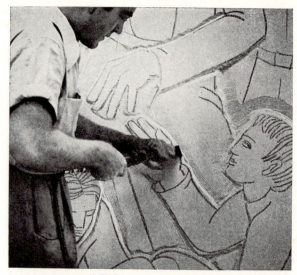

136

137

138

Carving a Relief

Carved reliefs in stone and wood contain the same problems of handling materials and visualizing as carving in the round. Figures 135-140 show one of a number of procedures for carving a relief panel in stone. The drawing on the face of the limestone slab (Figure 135) followed a small sketch in plasteline, and indicates the general two-dimensional pattern of the design. The carving was done with pneumatic tools. In the early stages of development, the tooth chisel was used for greater control of the relatively flat planes (Figure 136). The three large figures were conceived as the foreground level, projecting one inch from the background which was planned to be flush with the wall surface. A problem existed here which could not be solved convincingly in the small sketch: would a one-inch depth be sufficient to allow consistent modeling of the planes within this foreground level? This was answered by establishing the ratio of depth compression within the foreground figures before cutting into the background (Figure 137). When this ratio was established, the necessary depth of the background was found to be a little less than an inch, and the cutting proceeded rapidly and with confidence (Figure 138).

With the background plane established, visualization of the necessary indications of form and space became easier; large planes, which always control smaller planes, were carved freely but with enough definiteness to establish their functional capacity. Drawing was gradually de-emphasized and the manipulation of the planes was allowed to express the form as far as possible (Figure 139). Up to this point, claw tools of various sizes were used for nearly all the carving; as the shaping of the planes became more final, flat chisels were used in leveling and smoothing the background. Figure 140 shows the relief nearly completed with the background figures incised and planes and lines sharpened and accentuated.

The detail section of a high relief in polychromed mahogany (Figure 141) shows a type of form called silhouette relief. The figures occupy the entire thickness of the wood panel, and the wall upon which the relief is placed is the background plane. Notice how the perspective and tool strokes have been used to help the illusion of depth; these panels are but 2½ inches thick and the figures nearly life-size.

139

140

141

12· Waste Molding and Casting

WHILE molding and casting techniques are not creative processes in themselves, they have an important relationship to sculptural expression. Traditionally, sculptors have considered molding and casting an integral part of their art, and only in the current age of specialization have there been tendencies toward separating them from the creative process. A sculptor who understands these techniques will have more freedom of expression, more possibilities of direction, and more clarity of imagination than one whose hands are tied through lack of knowledge. True, the sculptor often better spends his time in purely creative work, leaving these mechanical matters to others, but unless he is sufficiently familiar with the processes to visualize the development of his sculpture and to control it to the finish, the final result—that which counts most—may fall short of his anticipations.

Molds are made of sculpture for one of two reasons: to transfer the form from one material to another or to make duplicate copies in the same material or other materials. Of the two, we are primarily interested in the first, though in some types of molds, both functions may be served. The waste mold, however, is used only for the former purpose; as its name implies, it is destroyed in the process of casting.

Waste molds are almost invariably made of plaster, though there are indications that some recently developed synthetic materials and low-melting metals may prove superior if they can be produced to sell at a reasonable price. Excellent molds can be made with plaster, provided the material and the technique of molding are understood; if not, many complications may arise, resulting in extra work and distortions of the cast. Because of the nature of the waste mold, the original model must be made of a plastic substance, such as clay, plasteline, or wax, which can be easily removed from the plaster mold. Clay that has become hard or dry is difficult to cast, and the mold often cracks or breaks in the process of removing it from the model. A hard model also prevents the use of the metal separating wall, described later.

Procedure for Making the Mold

The model (Figure 142), made of modeling clay, is studied carefully to find the simplest and most logical divisions, not only for the removal of the mold from the model but for its reassembly. In this case there will be a vertical division slightly back of the widest points, so that it will be possible to pull the back sections off without excessive strain on the plaster. The division is indicated with a very light line drawn on the clay. Along this line short strips of hard, thin shim brass or aluminum are pushed into the clay, making a continuous wall which will separate the parts of the mold (Figure 143). If this wall is slanted slightly toward the back of the model, the sections of the mold will register more accurately in reassembly. The armature support makes it necessary to divide the model horizontally in order to remove the mold. Considerable care should be taken with this metal wall. The pieces should enter the clay far enough to be firm and overlap each other just sufficiently to make the wall continuous. The junction of the metal and clay should be neat, and sharp angles should

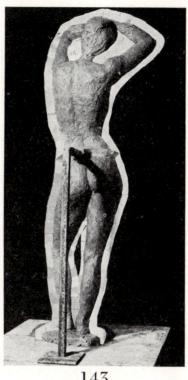
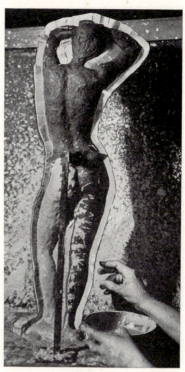

142   143   144

be avoided since they will result in fragile projections on the mold. The outside edge of the wall can be kept neat by trimming projecting corners with shears.

The first coat of plaster applied to the model should be about ⅛ inch thick; it is colored to indicate the proximity of the cast when the mold is eventually chipped off after casting. Usually, a small amount of bluing is put in the mixing water for this purpose. The plaster should be mixed a little heavy, since there is need of strength but not porosity. But it should not be so heavy as to make the fluid slurry too thick to enter the small crevices of the surface. A good rule is to add plaster until all the mixing water is used up and then to sprinkle a thin layer of plaster over this (see Chapter 5). When the plaster is thoroughly mixed and before it begins to thicken, it is flicked on the clay with the tips of the fingers (Figure 144). After a little experience the plaster can be thrown accurately and with enough force to make a true impression of the surface. It is best to start at the bottom and work upward so that there is no danger of plaster dripping and cov-

149

  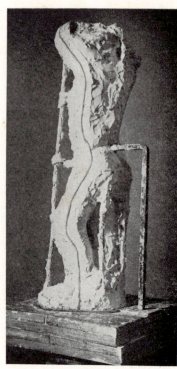

145 146 147

ering an area without being forced into the texture. If the plaster thickens before the model is covered with this first coat, a fresh mix of blue plaster should be made and the process continued. Remember that this first layer is very important and determines the surface of the final cast; if the plaster is mixed too heavy or too weak, much of the texture and detail will be lost, and if this colored layer is too thick, it will not serve the function of a dividing line.

When the entire model is covered with this thin blue coat, the excess plaster should be cleaned from the modeling board, but a rim of plaster should be left around the base the same width as the metal wall to indicate the thickness of the mold in this area (Figure 145). Next a layer of white plaster is applied in the same manner that the blue was thrown on the clay. Be sure not to leave air spaces. As this plaster thickens, it need not be thrown away but can be built up around the metal wall, if care is taken not to break the blue layer. When this mix of plaster has set, the wall will be strong enough so that it can be cleaned by scraping off the excess plaster crossing its edge (Figure 146).

This is very important since plaster crossing the wall binds the sections of the mold together and defeats the purpose of the wall.

At this stage, the mold is about ¼ or ⅜ inch thick. Before the next plaster is mixed metal or shellacked wood supports are cut to the proper length and placed against the mold where strength is needed. With the next batch of plaster, which can be enough to bring the mold to its finished thickness of from ½ to ¾ inch, these supports are attached to the mold with hemp fiber while the plaster is in the liquid stage. As the plaster becomes plastic, the final thickness of the mold is built up, a flat plane being maintained across the seam (Figure 147) to insure positive registration in reassembling.

Removing the Mold from the Model

When the plaster has set completely, the mold can be taken off the clay. The top part of the back (Figure 148) is easiest to remove since it has fewer large undercuts. An undercut is a section of a form so shaped that a mold cannot be pulled from it. A mold of a sphere, for instance, made in two pieces of identical size will not have an undercut, but if one piece is larger than the other it will curve around the sphere in such a way as to prevent its being pulled off; this extra part of the curve is referred to as an undercut. Vacuum between the plaster and the clay can be relieved by applying water to the section being pulled off and driving a blunt wedge, such as a cold chisel, a short way into the seam.

Figure 149 shows the two back sections of the mold which have little if any undercutting, and the relatively consistent thickness of the plaster. Rather than trying to pull the front section off, you should dig the clay out from the back (Figure 150) so that no unnecessary strain is applied to the mold. When all the clay has been removed the pieces of the mold are washed with water and a soft brush. A thin projection of plaster, resulting from the cut made when the metal pieces were pushed into the clay, is sometimes found on the inside edge of the seam. This should be removed carefully so as to prevent its forming a line on the cast.

151

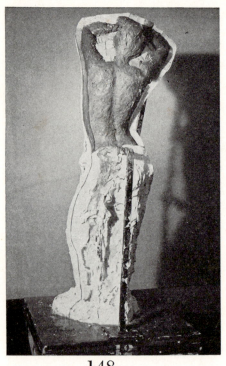

148

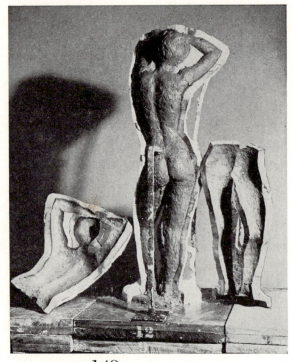

149

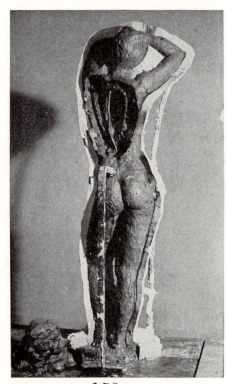

150

151

Casting the Waste Mold

A waste mold may be cast with any substance that is as hard or harder than plaster and does not involve heat in excess of 350° F. Some of these materials, such as cast stone, plastic, and oxychloride cements, are discussed in Chapter 15. In this case, the mold will be cast with molding plaster of the same type that was used in making the mold.

One of the most important aspects of molding and casting is the application of a separator to prevent materials from sticking to each other. Different casting materials require different separators; these are discussed in the chapters dealing with these materials. Plaster can be separated from plaster by any substance which waterproofs the mold: grease, oil, or wax. The choice of separators and the method of applying them depends on the degree of surface accuracy you desire on the cast. For rough casting, where the surface is not important, a coat of stearin wax thinned with warm kerosene applied over plaster which has been shellacked makes an excellent separator. A coat of vaseline over shellacked plaster also separates well, but in both cases most surface texture is filled with the separator and consequently does not cast. The most satisfactory separator for attaining an accurate surface on the plaster cast is green soap. This penetrates into the mold, sealing the pores and eliminating the necessity of the shellac coat. At the same time it leaves a very thin film of oil over the surface of the mold. The procedure for applying this soap is as follows:

1. Saturate the mold by soaking it in water.

2. Thin the green soap to a syrup consistency by mixing it with hot water.

3. Brush the soap over the inside of the mold vigorously, being careful not to damage the plaster (Figure 151).

4. Keep the lather rich but not stiff, adding water when it becomes thick and soap when it becomes thin.

5. Continue this process for about twenty minutes or until the surface of the mold becomes slick and oily, remembering that the soap is penetrating the plaster and must be added continually.

6. After the surface has become oily, hold the pieces of the mold under running water to remove the excess soap, being careful not to

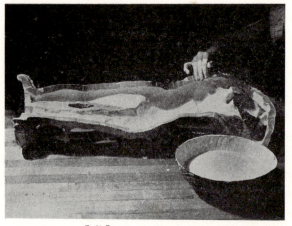

152

153

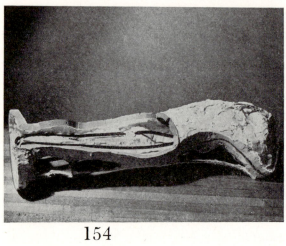

154

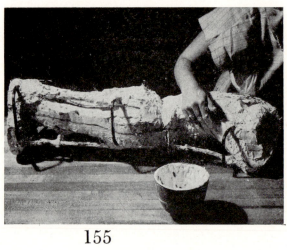

155

156

scrub off the oily film. If the surface is properly sealed, water will roll up into droplets on the surface; if not, additional soaping is necessary.

7. Any excess soap left in the mold will dry to a white film in a few minutes. This must be removed by brushing lightly with a dry brush. If left in the mold it interferes with the setting of the plaster and will cause "cheesy" areas on the cast.

There are two methods of casting a waste mold: by reassembling the mold and filling it, and by partially filling each piece separately before reassembly. In the first method there is little opportunity to reinforce the cast except for very simple forms, and there is also danger of the mold not filling completely or having a bad surface. The second method is better for the type of form illustrated here.

A small amount of liquid plaster mixed a little on the heavy side is poured into a section. Then the piece is picked up and rolled slowly so that the plaster runs over the entire inner surface, making a coating which will be the outer layer of the cast. A small amount of vibration will help get rid of air pockets and will force the plaster into the texture of the mold. When the surface has been covered, the remaining plaster is built up inside the piece, keeping the edge of the piece clean (Figure 152). This layer should be made at least ¼ inch thick, except in narrow openings such as the ankles and neck, so that there will be less danger of its flaking off the cast.

If the layer is beveled from the edge at a slight angle, there will be no chance of its bumping into the adjacent piece and holding the mold out of registration. Also, this will form a channel between the edges of the sections of the cast so that fresh plaster can run in and fill the joints.

Metal rods, which have been cut and bent to follow roughly the axes of the form, are laid in their proper positions and attached to the first layer of the cast with hemp fiber dipped in plaster (Figure 153). The most practical reinforcing metal is square rods of cold rolled steel; this is quite hard but malleable and the square sections make bending easier. Thinner steel rods can be used in the arms. To prevent rusting, these should be given a coat of shellac or lacquer and allowed to dry before using. Be sure there is sufficient room around

155

these supports for fresh plaster to run through; this may necessitate carving off some of the plaster previously added in the thin sections.

When all the pieces have been partially filled the edges of the mold should be checked again to see that there is no plaster on them which will prevent a close joint. The pieces are reassembled, and the halves of the registration plane which was made across the metal wall are matched (Figure 154). Clamps made by bending cold rolled steel into a broad U are used to hold the pieces together. They are driven onto the mold, and their spring tension pulls the pieces together tightly. They should be attached to the mold with bits of plaster-soaked fiber to prevent slipping. The outer area of the joint between the parts of the mold is then covered with plaster to keep the mold from leaking (Figure 155).

The last step is to turn the mold to a vertical position, upside down, and fill the remaining space inside the mold with plaster. In doing this, use the plaster immediately after mixing when it is thinnest and pour down one leg only, allowing air to escape through the other (Figure 156). When the fresh plaster rises into the other leg the mold is filled, though it is wise to lift the assembly and bump it lightly against the floor a few times to work out any air that may have been trapped inside. Large casts can be made hollow by pouring out the plaster in excess of what is necessary to build up the desired thickness.

Removing the Mold from the Cast

After the plaster has set completely, the mold is broken off the cast. The first step is to remove all the metal or wood reinforcements on the mold by tapping them with a hammer and pulling. In places it may be necessary to cut the fiber ties with a cold chisel. Then, starting on the joint at the top of the mold, break the plaster from the cast by driving the cold chisel into the mold at right angles, stopping at the blue layer of the mold to prevent cutting into the cast. Do not try to remove large pieces or there will be danger of cracking the cast, and do not carve the mold off—that takes too much time and is unnecessary since a thick piece can be broken off the cast as easily as a thin piece. Work from the top down, allowing the mold to strengthen the

157 158

cast against the chipping as long as possible (Figure 157). Most of the blue layer will come off with the rest of the mold but bits of it may stick in crevices of the cast; these can be removed with a pointed plaster tool.

If the mold has been properly fitted together, the seam at the joints will be a thin projection of plaster. Care in removing this is quite important, since haphazard cutting may emphasize the joint. Wherever possible the surrounding texture should be carried across the seam to give continuity to the contour.

A few air holes or nicks from the chisel make some patching inevitable. As mentioned in Chapter 5, regularly mixed plaster added to set plaster becomes harder and darker. The following procedure for preventing this is called "killing" plaster. A very thin mix of plaster is made: about two thirds as much plaster is used as in a regular mix. This is allowed to stand without stirring until the plaster begins to set under the excess water. Then it is stirred and built on the wet cast. When it sets, the color and hardness will be near that of the cast.

13· Plaster Piece Molds

A MOLD with sections completely free of undercuts is called a piece mold. This definition is more or less accurate depending on the nature of the materials involved in the original model and the cast. For instance, the first mold presented in this chapter is made from a stone model, the hardness of which eliminates the possibility of removing intact a section containing an undercut. On the other hand, the second mold, made from plastic clay, withstands slight undercutting without damaging the sections in removal, though there is some scarring of the model. When the second mold is cast in clay, there is sufficient shrinkage of the cast to compensate for these slight undercuts, but if it were cast in plaster they would bind and the sections would have to be broken. Piece molds have two advantages over waste molds: impressions can be made from models in a hard substance and a number of reproductions can be made from them. They have the one disadvantage of requiring considerably more time to make.

With sufficient time and planning, a piece mold can be made of any form, no matter how complex; intricate undercutting simply involves planning the proper number of pieces and a means of reassembling them accurately. We shall see from the demonstration here the major principles and reasoning processes involved in planning a piece mold.

The First Group

Taking as our model the stone carving in Figure 159, we study the form to find the logical grouping of the pieces. Here, as in most sculptures, the two sides offer the simplest arrangement. A more complicated shape might demand three groups of pieces or more, but every attempt should be made to restrict the groups to two because of the difficulty of handling more than two in casting. A line is drawn about midway between the two sides, the form laid horizontally, and a smooth sturdy floor of clay is built up to the dividing line (Figure 160). A board fastened tightly against the bottom of the base will serve later as a wall for that part of the mold. The pieces made from this exposed portion of the model, which will be the first group, are planned by studying the form carefully for undercuts and anticipating the removal of each piece. These sections are indicated by pencil lines and a wall of clay is built around the initial piece (Figure 161). The slant of this wall will later determine the order in which the pieces are removed from the model; a good system to follow is to slant the wall consistently inward so that the pieces can be removed in reverse of the order in which they were made.

To further waterproof the stone, which had been given a coat of shellac before embedding, the surface inside the clay wall is covered with a thin film of stearin melted down in kerosene and brushed on while warm. When cool, thick areas will appear white and can be picked up with a bristle brush. Stearin should not be applied outside the retaining wall since its presence would prevent the other clay walls from sticking to the stone.

The proportion of plaster to water should be about the same as for the waste mold, a little heavy, since this mold will eventually be filled with cast stone which requires strength rather than porosity. The

159

159

160

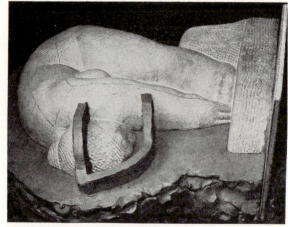

161

162

163

plaster is poured into the section while quite liquid and puddled with a modeling tool to bring trapped air to the top. When the plaster has set, the clay wall is removed and an adjacent section fenced off with clay, incorporating part of the edge of the previous piece in the wall (Figure 162). This plaster portion of the wall must be separated from the next pouring by a continuous film of stearin; shellacking is not necessary.

Elongated sections such as that shown in Figure 163 should be reinforced with hemp fiber and bent steel rods. This is done by first filling the section with plaster, allowing it to thicken, and carefully inserting the fiber and steel, keeping it toward the center of the piece.

When the entire group of pieces is finished (Figure 164), they should be numbered in reverse order to aid in remembering how to remove them. The next step is to make a containing form, called a shell, to hold these sections in place. This shell will be a one-piece mold of the group, and all undercuts on the outer surface of the pieces must be removed, tapering the sides slightly to avoid friction. A V groove is cut around each piece to register it properly in the shell as shown in Figure 165, and several hemispherical indentures about ½ inch in diameter are made on the clay floor for registration of the shell. The surface of the plaster is given a heavy coat of shellac, followed, when dry, by a relatively heavy coat of stearin; absolute accuracy here is not so important as being certain of easy removal of the shell. The shell is made by pouring a coat of plaster over the surface and building up with strips of fiber or burlap saturated with liquid plaster. A good shell should be thin, strong, and neat, having a flat plane at the top parallel to the bottom to aid in holding it upright for eventual casting (Figure 166).

The Second Group

The entire assembly—shell, pieces, model, and retaining floor—is turned over and the clay removed. The edges of the pieces and shell which will form the floor for the second group are shellacked, the boundaries of each section marked on the stone, and a wall built for the first piece (Figure 167). Before we proceed further, a problem of casting must

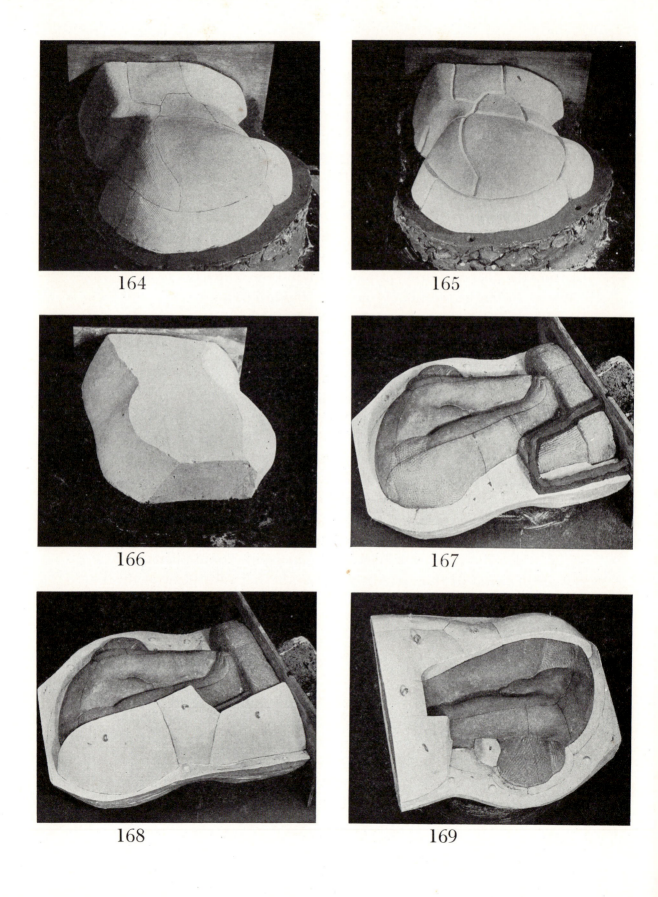

164

165

166

167

168

169

be foreseen and solved. When the mold is finished, the model removed, and the two groups are ready to put together, one must be lifted onto the other. It is necessary to have some means of holding these pieces to their shell. In each of the sections in this group, then, we will insert a small wire loop to use for this purpose (Figure 168). The ends of this loop must be bent and should be placed about ½ inch down in the plaster when it has set just enough to hold the wire in place.

Undercutting at times may be of such a nature as to require exceptionally small pieces such as that shown on the face of the form in Figure 169. This becomes a "piece within a piece" when it is covered by a larger section and attached to it in the same manner that the other pieces will be attached to the shell.

The same procedure used in making the first shell is followed for making the second, except that there must be openings in the shell through which the wire loops will be fastened. These are made by sticking conical shaped pieces of clay over the wire loops before making the shell (Figure 170). A registration plane, similar to that of the waste mold, is established across the joint between the two shells. The completed mold (Figure 171) is ready to open as soon as the final mix of plaster has set. The shell of one side is removed first and the pieces are taken out in the proper order, tapping lightly or using a stream of compressed air to help release them from the stone. As the pieces are removed they are reassembled in the shell (Figure 172). Strong rubber bands are attached to the wire loops of the second group as they are replaced in the shell. Each piece is pulled snugly into place and the bands held taut with wooden dowels or nails.

The unfastened group is laid horizontally, checking to see that the pieces fit properly in the shell, and the second group is placed in position on top of it. When these two halves are clamped or tied together the mold can be turned to the pouring position (Figure 173).

Casting the Piece Mold

To cast a mold of this kind in plaster, the same procedure used in casting the waste mold can be followed, except that instead of filling each

170

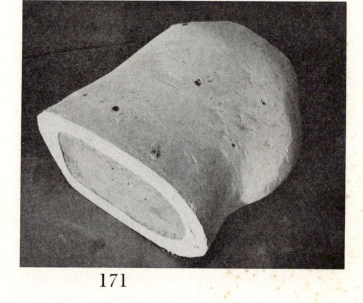

171

172

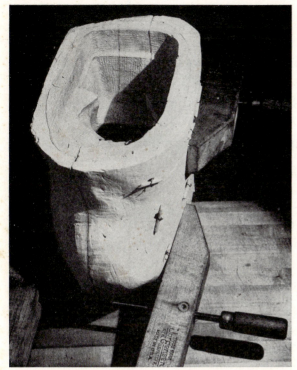 

173   174

piece, we build up a layer of plaster in each half. A cast as bulky as this one should be hollow and after putting the mold together and joining the halves, we pour out the excess plaster. Another method of casting in plaster and one that is especially adaptable to this mold is as follows:

1. After soaping the surface of the mold, assemble it and mix a batch of plaster about half the volume of the mold. Pour the plaster as soon as possible after mixing, tipping the mold slightly and running the plaster down the surface so as to avoid trapping air.

2. Lift the mold and pour out the plaster slowly, rotating the mold so that it flows over the entire surface, leaving a thin coating. This flowing action aids in getting a fine impression of the surface, preventing air pockets, and it controls the thickness of the layer of plaster.

3. Pour the plaster back into the mold and pour it out again in the same manner, depositing a second layer inside the mold. Repeat this process until the thickness increases to about one quarter of an inch, at which time the plaster will be too thick to use.

165

4. Cut strips of burlap about two by eight inches, saturate them with freshly mixed plaster, and build a layer around the inside of the cast. This greatly strengthens the cast.

5. Iron or wood supports can be built in both vertically and horizontally for additional strength.

When the plaster is hard, the mold is removed from the cast in the same manner as it was taken off the original model. If it has been properly soaped, the pieces can be removed easily, though compressed air or tapping with a wooden mallet may be necessary to break the suction. The unfinished plaster cast in Figure 174 shows the ridges made by the joints between the pieces. Many casts can be made from a good piece mold provided it is handled carefully, but eventually the pieces become too worn for further use.

A Piece Mold for Clay Casting

When a piece of sculpture is designed for reproduction, molding and casting problems should be taken into consideration. Simplification of form and elimination of unnecessary undercutting set limitations to the designing in the same way that the shape of a block of stone controls that which is carved in it. This design discipline need not curb the freedom of expression—it may well be a springboard for the creative imagination—but as in all techniques, the better the understanding of the possibilities and limitations of the problem, the freer the mind is to create.

Unlike the preceding problem, in which making the mold from the stone carving was an afterthought, the clay model in Figure 175 will be easy to mold and cast because it was designed specifically for that technique. If the form had not been planned for molding, if the model were in a hard material, or if it were to be cast in plaster instead of clay, the problem would be much greater and the resulting mold would be as complicated as the preceding one. Not that casting in plaster requires a complex mold—the form of the model for such a piece mold simply must be planned for that kind of casting.

166

175

176

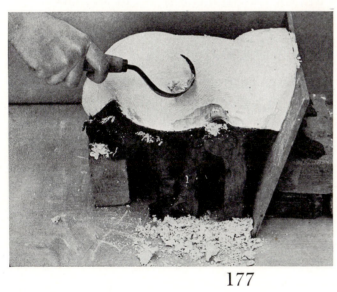

177

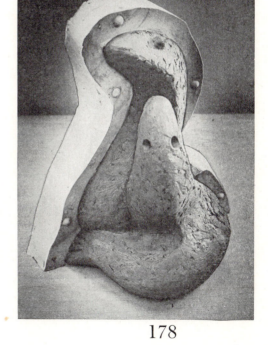

178

Making the Mold

The clay model is marked off into the necessary sections; in this case there are five including the bottom piece. Since a shell is not necessary, the floor and a retaining wall are built directly around the largest of these sections as shown in Figure 176. Care must be taken not to damage the model; clay which is softer than the model is used for the bed and the walls. The board at the bottom of the model is given a coating of thin clay-water solution. This prevents the wood from absorbing water from the mold and sticking. It is unwise to use stearin which seals the pores of the mold permanently and prevents proper absorption. Another check for undercuts should be made at this time, and it must be remembered that the shrinkage of the cast will compensate for only the very small ones. If a larger one has been overlooked, the floor will have to be shifted. Registration keys are cut into the clay floor.

The plaster for this mold should be porous since part of its function will be to absorb water from liquid clay. However, a certain amount of strength is necessary too, and a balance between these requires a ratio of water to plaster which is close to a normal mix (see page 51). A rule of thumb, accurate enough for this problem, is to add just sufficient plaster to use up all the mixing water. The plaster is poured while quite liquid, and puddled to work out the air pockets. If the mold is to be used regularly for a large number of casts, the pieces should be thick to increase the power of absorption. For moderate use, six or eight casts over a period of a month, a ¾-inch thickness is satisfactory for a mold of this size.

An important precaution in casting clay is to prevent chips of plaster from getting mixed in with the clay; after the clay is fired, any plaster chips in it will absorb moisture, expand, and crack the terra cotta. The outside of the mold should be neat and free of sharp edges and projections which might break off and fall into the mold. The clay retaining wall is removed and the surface smoothed by scraping (Figure 177).

The model is then lifted and the floor removed carefully. The edge of this first piece is painted with the thin clay-water mixture as a

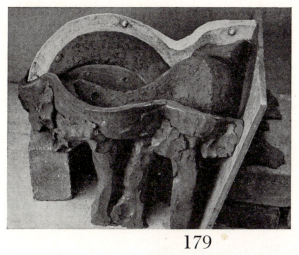

179

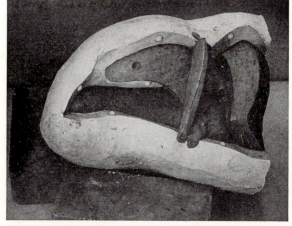

180

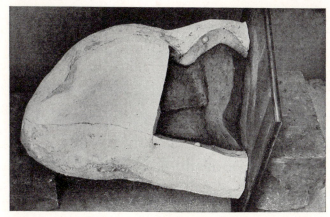

181

182

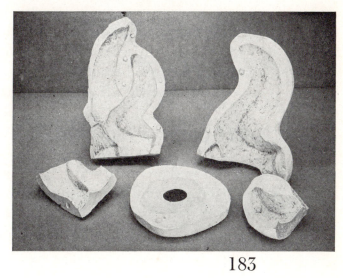

183

separator (Figure 178). The other pieces are poured in the same manner as the first, and care must be taken to use the same proportion of plaster to water for each piece (Figures 179-181). When the vertical sections are completed, the assembly is turned upside down, the bottom leveled, and a clay retaining wall built for the bottom piece. A piece of clay, tapering toward the bottom of the model, is placed in the center to form an opening through this piece (Figure 182).

The sections of the mold are then carefully removed from the model, washed with water, and put aside to dry (Figure 183). This may take from several days to two weeks depending on the thickness of the mold and moisture condition of the air.

Casting a Piece Mold with Slip

The dried pieces are put together and bound with strong cord or rubber bands (Figure 184). If the mold has become exceptionally dry, dampening the inside surface slightly before assembling will prevent areas of the cast from sticking to the mold because of a too sudden absorption of water.

The clay slip, which should be about the consistency of a normal mix of plaster before it starts to thicken, is made in the following manner:

1. A container, preferably a galvanized pail or stoneware crock, is half filled with water and the dry, powdered clay sifted into it, removing lumps, until the clay builds up slightly above the water.

2. This is left, without stirring, for at least an hour, allowing the particles of clay to become saturated.

3. The mixture is then stirred until it has an even consistency. If the slip is made from natural clay which has not been cleaned, it is necessary to strain it through an 18-mesh screen to remove large particles of foreign matter.

4. After thorough stirring, the mixture is left to stand overnight, or longer if possible, since aging improves the quality of the slip. The clay will settle and clear water will be found on top of the slip. Some or all of this water may be picked up with a sponge if the slip is too thin.

170

184   185

5. Before it is poured, the slip should be stirred thoroughly and vibrated to remove air.

The slip mixture is poured in a steady stream into the mold (Figure 185), and brought up even with the outer surface of the bottom piece. Almost immediately, the effect of absorption can be noticed: the slip will thicken next to the surface of the mold. Additional slip is added as its volume decreases from absorption. The mold is kept completely full but not overflowing. After a few minutes the mold is tipped so that the thickness of the layer of clay deposited on the surface of the mold can be seen clearly (Figure 186). When this reaches the proper thickness, about a quarter of an inch in this case, the excess slip is poured back in the container.

The clay in the mold is now much too soft to permit removal of the pieces; it must be left for several hours to become hard enough to support its own weight. As it hardens, more water is drawn into the mold or evaporated inside the cast, causing it to shrink and pull away

171

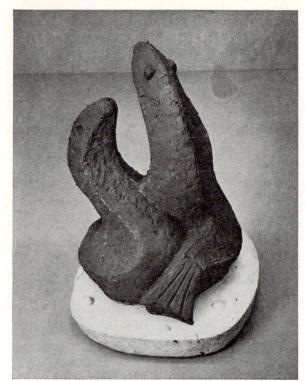

186   187

from the mold. If the pieces are of the same porosity, thickness, and dryness, this drying will be consistent and can be judged by the clay in the bottom opening, although it will be necessary to make some allowance for the additional evaporation at that point.

When the cast is hard enough, the lip of clay inside the pouring opening is cut away, as it is an undercut, and the mold turned bottom down. While the vertical pieces are being removed, one must be careful not to strain the relatively weak cast. It may be left on the bottom piece until quite hard, but in the meantime the projections on the seams should be removed and any air holes or marred areas patched with clay of the same body and consistency as the cast (Figure 187). When thoroughly dry, it is fired, as described in Chapter 8. The mold can be cast again immediately if sufficiently dry; dryness can be tested by putting a drop of slip on one of the pieces and observing the absorption.

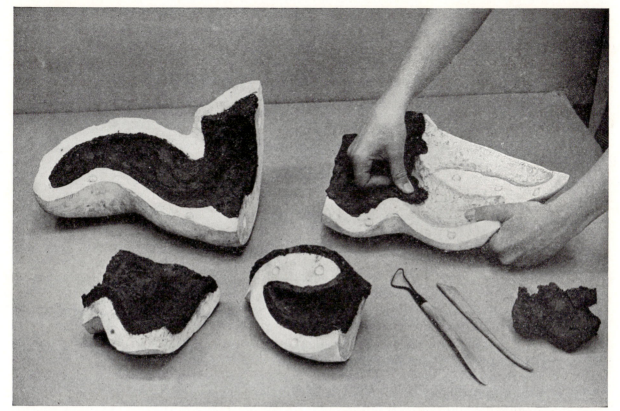

188

189

190

Pressing a Piece Mold with Clay

There is necessarily some distortion in a casting made with slip because of shrinkage; and there is also an inevitable "softness" of the surface texture, due to lack of force in bringing the clay up against the mold. By putting forth a little more effort, we can make a much more accurate casting by pressing plastic clay into the mold. As there is less water to get rid of, there will be less shrinkage, and a better texture will result from pushing the clay against the surface of the mold. Another advantage is that we can use grog in the clay to lessen shrinkage still further and to make a stronger cast. Grog cannot be used in slip because it is impossible to keep it evenly suspended in the solution.

The grog mix which is described in Chapter 4 should be about the right consistency for use in modeling. Begin at one spot on each piece, pressing the clay with the thumb against the mold, always adding new clay on top of that which has been applied so as not to form junction lines on the surface. Pressure on the clay causes it to flow outward and works the bits of clay together (Figure 188).

The clay is built up to a thickness of from one-quarter to one-half inch, and the edges of each piece are beveled slightly outward—the opposite of that done in casting the waste mold—and then brushed with water until sticky. When the pieces are put together this extra clay holds them slightly apart, but when they are pressed into position, the pieces of the cast become well joined. The bottom piece of the mold is not needed in this procedure, and when the other pieces are bound together, additional pressure can be applied against the mold by reaching down inside the cast with a modeling tool (Figure 189). With a dry mold and clay of normal consistency, the pieces can be removed almost immediately from the cast (Figure 190).

14· Flexible Molds

EACH of the molds described so far has a particular function, serving at least one purpose better than other kinds of molds. The waste mold is the simplest method of making a unique cast in a hard substance from a clay model, and the plaster piece mold is the most practical way of making clay casts. Flexible molds made of pliable substances make the solutions of complex undercutting problems simpler than piece molding, but they are not satisfactory for clay casting. There are certain other limitations in the use of flexible molds which are determined by the nature of the material used in the mold.

Materials for Flexible Molds

The major requirement for a flexible molding material is the property of being easily brought to a thin liquid and then set to a more or less stable rubber-like mass without excessive shrinkage. There are many substances suitable for flexible molds. Of these, we will investigate only those having distinct advantages for a particular casting problem, taking into consideration accuracy, ease of handling, and cost.

1. Gelatin or Glue

A refined animal glue. Standard quality for molds is known as number one technical grade. Obtainable in flake or powder form. Soaked in water, it becomes a greatly expanded rubbery mass which melts to a syrup-like viscosity in a double boiler. Gels slowly as it cools, congealing to an elastic mass at about 100° F. Advantages: takes a reasonably accurate surface impression; easy to melt; poured at low temperature of about 120° F; economical, can be remelted many times if a small amount of fungicide such as zinc sulfate or carbolic acid is added and if the mold is cut into small cubes and dried thoroughly after use. Disadvantages: some shrinkage in cooling to the gelled state; considerable shrinkage and warpage from evaporation of water; surface softens at temperatures as low as the exothermic heat of setting plaster.

2. Koroseal Flexible Molding Compound

Trade name for a rubber-like plastic (plasticized polyvinyl chloride). Melts to a pouring viscosity at from 260° F to 350° F. Available in several varieties for specific casting needs, some particularly suited to casting in plastics. Advantages: relatively accurate; does not require surface treatment for casting; strong durable substance with great elasticity; withstands surface temperatures of 160° F without softening; can be remelted repeatedly. Disadvantages: shrinkage in cooling; contraction must be controlled with heat; more difficult to melt than gelatin; more expensive than gelatin; cannot be poured over a model containing moisture; model should be heated to obtain free flow of compound.

3. Elastomer No. 105, Formulation No. 17

Trade name for a rubber-like vinyl compound. Obtained in liquid state ready for pouring. Polymerizes by heat at 220° F. Advantages: relatively accurate; does not require surface treatment for casting; withstands up to 200° F without softening; particularly suited to casting with plastics; can be either poured or built up; can be reinforced with cloth; requires no mixing. Disadvantages: some shrinkage in cooling; requires heating model and containing form or shell to 220° F; cannot be reused.

4. Rubber Latex Composition

Natural sap from the rubber tree, mixed with vulcanizing agents such as sulfur, and suspended in water and ammonia. Hardens by evaporation of moisture. Applied to the model by brushing. Can be used with fillers such as clay, wood flour, or cellucotton. Advantages: accurate surface impression; very elastic and tough; withstands 250° F; economical. Disadvantages: tendency toward excessive shrinkage and warpage; should be cured at 250° F (though this is not always necessary); lengthy molding procedure; surface of mold must be coated with a separator.

5. Perma-Flex Cold Molding Compound

Trade name for a synthetic rubber. Furnished in liquid state and set by the addition of two curatives. Available in a number of modifications with various toughnesses and setting times. Advantages: extremely accurate; no perceptible expansion or shrinkage since setting is chemical and does not involve heat or evaporation; no separator required for plaster or cast stone; can be poured like gelatin or brushed on like latex (while not so strong as Koroseal FMC or as elastic as latex, it has enough of these properties to fulfill most flexible molding needs); can be reinforced with cheesecloth so as to make a very strong, thin mold; can be stored for years without dimensional change; speed of setting can be controlled precisely from a few minutes to several hours by varying the amounts of the curatives; can be partially reclaimed by grinding scraps and using them as a filler in a fresh mix. Disadvantages: separator required in casting plastics such as phenolic resins and polyesters; more expensive than the above materials.

There is no perfect molding material—all have certain disadvantages along with their advantages, but there is enough variety in the five above to permit us to find a nearly perfect material for any casting problem. The advantages and disadvantages listed are general and within a specific mold may be trivial. The loss of surface quality due to the use of separators may not be a major factor in a large piece or one whose surface will be worked over after casting. Also, care in the application of separators can prevent excessive alteration of the surface.

177

The problem of shrinkage is of variable importance, too, and can often be reduced to a minimum by judicious handling. In using gelatin, for instance, less water in the mix reduces the potential of shrinkage from evaporation and pouring the gelatin at the lowest temperature at which it will flow properly eliminates unnecessary shrinkage from heat loss. The problem becomes one of balancing shrinkage against accuracy of surface impression.

Selecting a flexible molding material requires an evaluation of the problem at hand, and the decision is made with consideration for both aspects of the problem—that is, the making of the mold and its casting. Koroseal FMC, for instance, cannot be poured successfully against a wet plaster model because its melting point is well above the boiling point of water; yet its properties may so well suit the casting problem that, rather than use another material, we may find the additional chore of drying the model worth while. In a similar manner, the ease of handling gelatin in making a mold may be completely offset by the difficulty and limitations of casting with it.

Along with the explanation of the two following procedures for making and casting flexible molds, we will discuss more specific problems of using these materials.

Most flexible molds require a supporting outer mold or shell to hold them in place while being cast. The two types of flexible molds which we will refer to as the *poured mold* and the *built-up mold,* are distinguished by whether the molding material is poured into a preformed shell, or built up on the model and the shell made afterward.

Separators

The first step in both procedures is the preparation of the model. Moist clay and wax do not need separators, but the surfaces of all hard substances such as dried clay, plaster, and stone must be sealed thoroughly to prevent sticking of the molding material. There are several separators which may be preferable to the shellac-stearin-kerosene combination described in the preceding chapter. A 50-50 mixture of castor oil and alcohol makes a good separator over a shellacked surface. Beeswax, heated to about 160° F and thinned with carbon tetrachloride, or stearin melted in hot carbon tetrachloride, is also satisfactory for forming a film over a hard surface. The latter two are noninflammable and are preferable to similar hot mixtures using kerosene. The viscosity of the separator and the amount applied should be controlled by the porosity of the model. In all cases the surface must be adequately sealed without excessive use of the separator. A little experience will enable you to tell by feel when the model is properly prepared. If in doubt, always make a test with the same materials and conditions.

Procedure for Making a Poured Mold

The following demonstration is of a mold made from a plaster model with Cold Molding Compound (CMC). As in the initial step of making a shell piece mold, the form is divided into logical sections for the shell. Here, as usual, two sections are necessary, but small simple models may require only one, and complex models, three or more. Since the shell is to be made before the CMC is poured, the first step is to build up in clay the space for the molding material and to make the shell over it, removing the clay later.

The plaster model, having been brushed with a light coat of shellac, is put into a clay bed and a clay floor is built up, leaving the first section exposed (Figure 191). This floor should be well supported from underneath, particularly next to the model, since a leak here could cause great difficulty and might ruin the entire pouring. The floor is made as neatly as possible, and beveled slightly inward; a registration groove is cut in it about ½ inch from the model (Figure 192). Strips of clay ½ inch thick are laid across the form, and the clay is pressed down in the hollow areas without altering the thickness of the strips (Figure 193). A ridge is built up on top of the outer edge of these clay strips to help hold the molding material in place. Another groove is cut ½ inch out from this ridge to insure alignment of the parts of the shell. The inner groove under the clay strips serves the same function for the two sections of the molding material. The clay, representing the space for the molding material, is made of even thickness, and its surface is kept free of undercuts. Three small cylinders

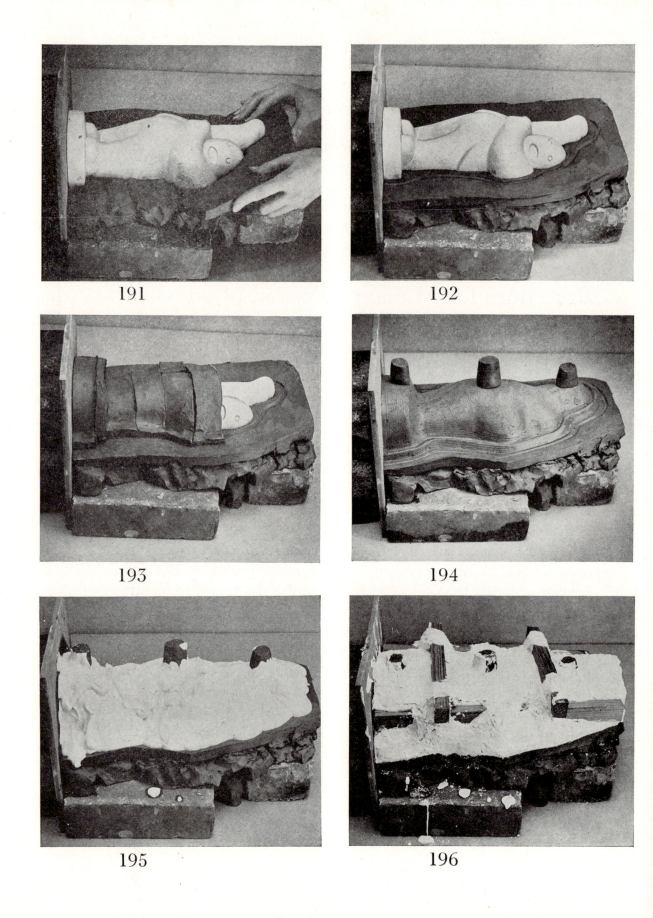

191

192

193

194

195

196

of clay are set on the highest points to form openings in the shell for pouring and venting (Figure 194). It is helpful to keep an accurate check on the volume of clay used in covering the model, as that is the volume of material necessary to fill this section of the shell.

The plaster shell should be about ¾ inch thick and made quite strong. Use a heavy mix of plaster and reinforce it with hemp fiber (Figure 195). Place shellacked wood strips strategically and anchor them with fiber and plaster (Figure 196).

The first half of the shell is lifted off and the clay covering removed carefully from the model without damaging the floor (Figure 197). The inside of the shell section is shellacked and rubbed with vaseline until the surface is greasy. The model is brushed with the castor oil-alcohol solution, which forms a thin but continuous film of oil over its surface. Using the grooves as guides, replace the shell over the model. Seal all joints with clay and make funnels with soft sheet aluminum, inserting them in the openings of the shell as shown in Figure 198.

The Cold Molding Compound is obtained as three separate ingredients, Syrup A, Curative B, and Catalyst C. There are several varieties of Syrup A, of which that known as Blak-Tufy is best suited to this kind of problem. It is prepared in the following manner:

1. Weigh accurately the volume of Syrup A equal to the volume of space inside the shell and funnels, using a round straight-sided container such as an ice cream carton or a can with the top removed.

2. Add to this 15 percent of Curative B and 1.5 percent of Catalyst C, being as accurate as possible in weighing.

3. Mix immediately, stirring with a flat piece of wood similar to a ruler, and scraping the sides and bottom of the container to be sure of uniform mixing.

4. Avoid as far as possible the entrapping of air, and when the mixture is thoroughly mixed, vibrate the compound to remove bubbles made while stirring.

The compound is poured immediately after preparation. The central funnel is used as a pouring point, and the shell is filled until the compound rises in the vents (Figure 199). Projecting portions of

181

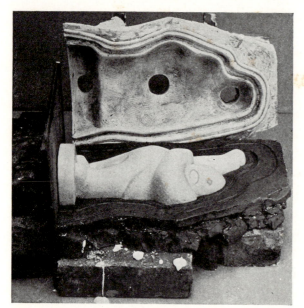

197

198

199

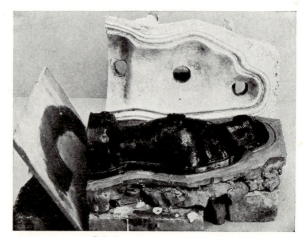

200

some models may make it necessary to tilt the assembly slightly to avoid trapping air.

At normal temperatures, 75° F to 95° F, this proportion of CMC ingredients will remain fluid for about thirty minutes and will cure completely in six to eight hours. Adding larger amounts of the B and C decreases this time considerably; a maximum is reached with the proportion 100A:25B:4C, which is fluid from three to five minutes and cures in thirty to forty minutes. Increasing the temperature will further hasten the setting time.

When the compound has cured, the shell may be removed to see if any trapped air has prevented complete filling (Figure 200). If an air hole seems sufficiently large to weaken the mold, it can be filled as follows: clean the separator from around the hole, drill through the shell immediately above it, replace the shell after covering the raw plaster with separator and fill the cavity with a new mix of compound. The new material will bond perfectly with the cured mold provided no grease or oil is on the surface.

Turning the assembly over and cleaning away the clay, the process of making and filling the shell is repeated for the other section (Figures 201-205). There are a few differences, however: no additional registration grooves are needed; the floor, which is now the compound and the shell, has ridges made by the grooves in the first floor (Figure 201). The second clay covering is kept the same thickness as the first and made with a similar overlapping ledge to hold the compound in its shell (Figure 202). The edge of the first section of the shell and the base board are shellacked and coated with a film of vaseline.

When the second part of the shell is hard, it is removed, shellacked and coated thinly with vaseline. The edge of the cured compound is shellacked and given the same thin but continuous film of oil applied to the model. Be careful not to skip areas, since these would become joined with the fresh compound.

The two shells and base board are clamped firmly together, as shown in Figure 204, and filled with CMC. After this second pouring has cured, the two halves of the shell are removed (Figure 205) and the sections of the mold pulled carefully from the model. Since there is no shrinkage and the compound is in absolute contact with the model,

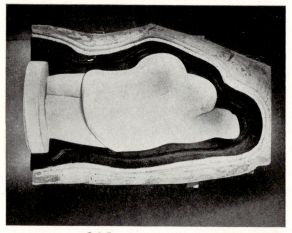

201

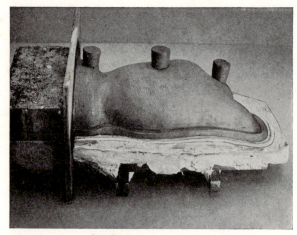

202

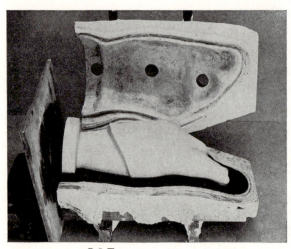

203

204

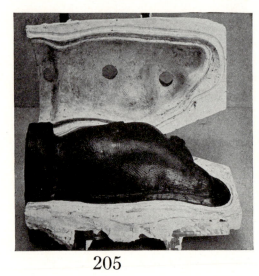

205

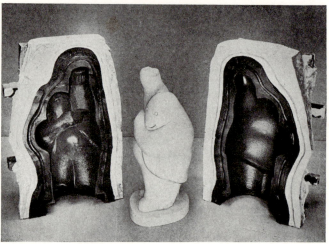

206

stripping must be very slow. A jet of compressed air is helpful in removing the compound. The oil from the separator is washed off with alcohol and the mold placed in its shell (Figure 206).

A mold made with Cold Molding Compound can be cast immediately, since it requires no preparation for plaster, wax, or cast stone. The mold may be cast in plaster with either of the methods described in casting a piece mold. It is extremely accurate; casts made from a good mold have little if any seam to work over. The material is strong and flexible and withstands temperatures in excess of 250° F. It can be stored indefinitely without deformation, since it is nonvolatile and chemically inert below 250° F.

The procedure for making a gelatin mold is the same as the above except it should be made twice as thick. The gelatin is prepared in the following manner:

1. The gelatin is cut into small cubes, covered with water, and left to soak about twelve hours.

2. All water not absorbed by the gelatin is drained off.

3. The softened gelatin is melted in a double boiler.

4. A teaspoonful of carbolic acid per gallon of melted gelatin or 1 percent zinc sulfate by weight is added to prevent mildew and organic decomposition.

5. When completely melted, air bubbles and scum are removed, and it is allowed to cool to about 120° F before pouring.

As mentioned before, the less water added to the gelatin, the more stable the mold will be; if part (up to 75 percent) of the water used for soaking the gelatin is replaced by a 50-50 mixture of glycerin and sorbitol, there will be less shrinkage from evaporation and the quality of the mold will be greatly improved. Also, the cooler the mixture is poured, short of becoming too viscous, the better. Common practice is to pour as soon as the finger can be held in the gelatin for a short time. This, of course, varies with different mixtures of gelatin and for different problems of molding.

When the gelatin has cooled to room temperature, its edge, against which the second section of the mold will be poured, must be coated with wax or vaseline and dusted with talc to separate the halves. The second pouring must not be too hot, lest it melt the first part of the mold and join to it.

A gelatin mold should be cast as soon as possible. When it is removed from the model, brush the surface with a strong solution of alum and water (10 percent alum, 90 percent water) to make it tougher, being careful not to leave pools of the solution which would warp the surface. After this, apply a thin layer of stearin-kerosene separator, brushing and picking up the excess with a bristle brush. The best method of casting plaster in this mold is as follows:

1. Assemble the mold and fill with plaster mixed with ice water.

2. Pour the plaster back in the mixing bowl, shaking the mold to break air bubbles.

3. Refill the mold with the same plaster, and, if possible, add reinforcements by working them down in the cast, keeping them away from the surface of the mold.

4. As soon as the plaster hardens and before it begins to get warm, quickly remove the mold.

Mixing the plaster with cold water helps greatly in reducing the heat built up during recrystallization, but even when mixed in this manner, the plaster will become hot enough to melt the surface of the gelatin if allowed to set completely in the mold. If the gelatin is brushed with a 2 to 4 percent formaldehyde-water solution instead of the alum solution, the mold will better withstand the heat of setting plaster. However, gelatin thus treated is not remeltable.

For making the mold with Koroseal FMC the same general procedure is followed except in preparing the model, melting the material, and controlling the cooling and contraction of the mold. Before beginning, the plaster model is heated at 150° F until free of uncombined moisture. While the surface is hot, it is brushed with floor wax as long as the wax penetrates the plaster. A good grade of paste wax or a carnauba wax emulsion (sold as self-polishing wax) should be used. This process is repeated, and the model is then heated a third time to remove any moisture from the wax. The surface of the model is polished, and before pouring the mold, it is given a light coating of castor oil. The Koroseal FMC will take a better impression if the model is heated just before the pouring; but that possibility is ruled out in using the above technique, since half of the model is embedded in clay. However, in making a one-piece Koroseal FMC mold or by using the method suggested for pouring Elastomer 105 (described next), the model can be hot when the material is poured.

Koroseal FMC must be melted in an enameled or stainless steel container at a temperature of from 260° F to 350° F, depending on the particular type being used. The best heating device for this purpose is an electric roaster and radiant broiler similar to that described on page 216. Small amounts can be melted under heat lamps or over a direct flame covered with an asbestos pad. In the latter case the material must be stirred continuously.

It is very important not to overheat Koroseal FMC; if any part becomes burnt, remove it immediately as a small amount of burnt material will ruin the entire melt. Overheating is first indicated by excessive smoking and discoloration of the honey-colored material. The Koroseal FMC should be poured as soon as it is completely melted and air bubbles disappear from the top.

Much of the shrinkage from cooling can be counteracted by keeping the material in the pouring funnel and vents fluid as long as possible, and by allowing the material to cool first at the surface of the model. Radiant heat lamps, properly placed, serve this function very well. The second pouring must be separated from the first by a light but continuous film of oil.

Koroseal FMC makes a very strong elastic mold which will keep indefinitely. It will not soften at temperatures below 160° F and needs no separator for plaster, wax, cast stone, or plastics such as phenolic resins and polyesters.

Elastomer 105 can be used only when the entire mold assembly can be heated to 220° F after pouring. To do this requires some adjustment in the procedure described above. First, the model is attached firmly to a base board and placed in an upright position. Then, both halves of the shell are made simultaneously, by covering the entire model with the proper thickness of clay and by using metal strips to separate the two sections of the shell. The pouring opening and vents should be on the highest points. Before the shell is opened a mark is made around it on the base board so as to be able to return it to the same position. The clay is removed and the model prepared as for the Koroseal FMC mold. The shell, which has been given a heavy coat of paste floor wax, is replaced around the model and fastened to the base. All joints are sealed by covering them completely with a thin layer of plaster. This assembly is heated in an oven for thirty minutes at 220° F. It is removed and the space between the shell and model filled with Elastomer 105, which comes as a liquid ready for pouring.

The mold is then returned to the oven and heated about twenty minutes more—ten minutes for each ¼ inch of thickness. When the mold is cool, the shell is removed by cutting off the plaster at the joints. Since plaster is weakened when heated above 150° F, the shell will be somewhat more fragile than it was before heating. If the mold is to be used for a large number of casts, a new shell can be built over the set Elastomer and the old shell can be thrown away. The Elastomer is now in one piece covering the entire model. It is cut at the seam of the shell with a sharp glue knife, a knife with the side of its blade bent to a U near the point; this makes a tongue-and-groove joint in the molding material. A mold made with Elastomer 105 has properties similar to those of Koroseal FMC.

Latex compounds are not suited to the pouring procedure, since they must be applied in thin layers, and each layer allowed to dry partially before adding the next. This material is discussed in the following section.

The Built-up Mold

The quickest, though not necessarily the best, way to make a flexible mold is by the built-up method. If we examine further the nature of a flexible mold, we see that actually the function of the flexible portion is to reduce the undercuts of the model to a simple piece mold, which is the shell. In other words the pliable materials serve as a transition from the complex model to the simple shell. If the model has many deep undercuts this transition material will have to be quite thick in

188

places to make a suitable shell; on the other hand, if the undercutting consists mostly of roughly textured surface and small accents, only a thin layer of flexible material is needed. Usually, the best way to make a thick mold is by pouring; the best way to make a thin one is by building up.

Latex, Cold Molding Compound, and Elastomer 105 can be built up on a model. Of the three, CMC is the most satisfactory for average molding because of its accuracy and the speed and simplicity of making the mold. Elastomer 105 is a little more difficult to handle but makes an excellent mold especially for casting in plastics. Latex is the cheapest of the materials but lacks the accuracy and stability of the other two and requires considerably more time to make a mold. In the following procedure CMC is built up on a moist clay model (Figure 207); adaptations of the process for the other materials are described later.

A small amount of CMC is mixed using a proportion of 100A:20B:2.5C by weight. As soon as this is thoroughly mixed it is brushed over the model, starting from the bottom to avoid loose runs that might trap air (Figure 208). If possible the model may be tilted to help in covering overhanging surfaces. Press strips of cheese-cloth gently into the CMC, being careful that they become saturated and an integral part of the layer (Figure 209). Handle the CMC as neatly as possible; avoid getting it on the hands and clothes; before curing it can be removed with toluene, but once it is set it is nearly insoluble.

Raising the temperature of the CMC with an infra-red lamp, as shown in Figure 210, is not necessary, but it helps in two ways: the heat thins the compound momentarily, enabling it to take a more accurate impression of the model's surface, and it speeds up the curing of the coating. With a little experience, you can learn to mix a larger quantity of material and, by applying heat to the model, build up several layers from one batch. Additional material can be added as soon as that underneath thickens enough to hold the new layer in place.

Reinforced with cheesecloth, CMC molds need not be more than ⅛ inch thick as far as strength is concerned. However, the necessity of reducing the undercutting for a two-piece shell and widening the

207

208

209

210

211

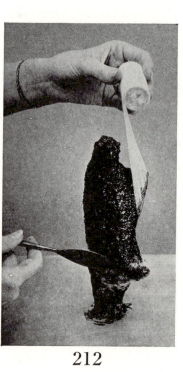

212

mold at the seam to make a good joint requires additional building up in places. Scraps of cured CMC, preferably those without reinforcement, can be ground in a meat chopper and mixed with fresh CMC to make a thick granular paste.

This is built on the mold with a plaster spatula (Figure 211) and covered with cheesecloth as in Figure 212 to make an even surface. To further smooth the surface and insure complete saturation of the cloth, a final mix of CMC may be painted over the mold.

A quick method of making a shell is shown in Figures 213 and 214. Metal strips cannot be pushed into the CMC. Instead of building a clay wall at the joint and making each half separately, plaster is built over the mold and cut with a previously embedded string. The string should be waxed, should be placed along the widest part of the ridge built up on the mold, and stuck to the CMC with small bits of wax so that the ends are kept accessible (Figure 213). A heavy mix of plaster is then built over the mold to a thickness of about ½ inch. When this passes the plastic stage so that the plaster will not flow back together and before it gets very hard, the string is pulled at a right angle away from the CMC, cutting the shell into sections (Figure 214). Additional plaster and fiber may be built over these sections by inserting metal strips in the cut to keep them separate. After removing the shell, the CMC is cut with a sharp glue knife into two sections corresponding to the shell (Figure 215).

The completed mold (Figure 216) does not have the neat appearance of the poured mold but it is just as accurate, producing casts with minute seams and excellent surface reproduction. This kind of mold can be made in from two to three hours. A variation on this method, requiring a little more time and work but producing a neater mold, is a combination of the two procedures, the poured and built-up. Building a retaining wall at the joint with the necessary registration grooves, one section of the CMC mold is built-up and its shell made. Then the clay wall is removed and the mold is completed by building the other sections of the mold and shell, being sure to use separators.

In molding small pieces it is often possible to use a one-piece shell, shaping the mold conically so that there are no undercuts between it and the shell. Also, it may not be necessary to use a grooved glue knife

191

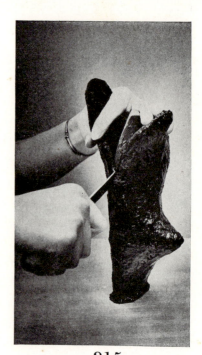

213

214

215

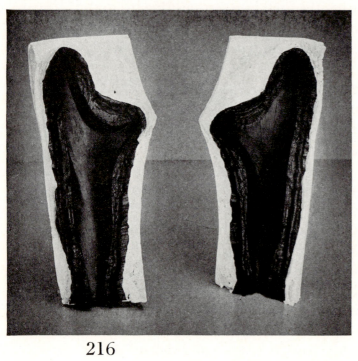

216

217

or to cut the mold into sections. In many cases, a smooth cut with a razor blade halfway around the mold is enough to allow removal of the model and casts and will give positive registration. This type of mold is sometimes called a coat mold.

There are two ways of handling latex in this procedure: it may be built up in one piece and cut into sections with a razor blade (the glue knife is unsatisfactory for latex), or the combination procedure, mentioned above, may be followed and each section built up separately. Although it takes more time, the latter is preferable, since better registration is possible. The latex is applied to the moist model in a series of thin layers, allowing each to dry until its milky appearance begins to change and the surface is tacky. This requires from thirty to forty-five minutes but can be speeded up if warm air such as that from an electric heater is blown over the mold. About eight of these layers are necessary to build up a ⅛-inch thickness, the minimum for proper strength. For filling undercuts, a paste made of equal parts of latex and a filler such as cellucotton or wood flour is built up in ⅛-inch layers, allowing each to dry enough to support the next. A tongue-and-groove ridge for registration of the mold in the shell is also built up with this paste. The shell is made in the same manner as that for the CMC built-up mold.

An uncured latex mold of this kind can be used successfully for a few casts made shortly after the mold is finished. The material takes an accurate impression of a surface and is very strong and elastic; but its excessive shrinkage and consequent warpage prevents it from making a completely satisfactory mold. If the model is free of moisture, the latex can be cured before making the shell by drying it thoroughly at 135° F for several hours and then raising and holding the temperature to 250° F for one hour. This makes the material more stable, and prevents further shrinkage and hardening.

Elastomer 105 works very well with the built-up procedure, but it has the one handicap of requiring a model free of moisture. If the model is of dried clay or plaster and an oven with controlled heat is available, the following procedure is fast, simple, and very satisfactory. The model is attached to a base with a small amount of the liquid Elastomer and heated at 220° F for a few minutes. It is removed from the oven and while it is still hot the material is brushed or poured over the form; or better still, the model may be dipped in the Elastomer. One of the advantages of this material is that it remains liquid until heated above 200° F and requires no mixing. Thus there is little waste if it is poured into a container large enough to allow dipping the model. When the model is coated, it is returned to the oven for three or four minutes to set the Elastomer and the dipping or brushing is continued. Cheesecloth can be saturated with the material and wrapped around the mold for strength and wads of it used to fill undercuts and build up the registration ridge. A ⅛-inch thickness of the cloth-reinforced material is sufficient in the thinnest areas of the mold. After completing the building up, the mold is left in the oven for ten or fifteen minutes at a temperature of 220° F for final curing. The shell can be made by any of the above methods and the mold cut with a razor blade or very sharp glue knife.

15· Cements and Plastics

TWO GROUPS of materials, cements and plastics, are treated together in this chapter. Although chemically and physically they belong in different categories, from our standpoint they have much in common. Both are relatively new, exciting materials undergoing constant development; both are well suited to the sculptor's casting problems; and neither has been given much opportunity in sculptural expression, being considered primarily as imitations or substitutes for other materials.

The first step in learning to work with these materials, as with all others, is to understand their natures; this, of course, is best learned through actual contact and experimentation. The following discussion does not attempt to evade this fact but is offered as general information with a few suggestions for specific applications of these materials to sculptural problems.

Cements

In sculpture, cements and the various mixtures made with them, such as concrete, are usually called *cast stone*. This name may be misleading if taken literally; the material should not be thought of as a means of arriving at a stone form by modeling and casting. We will do better perhaps to think of it as a hard, reinforceable substance with which to cast, its nature being closer to that of clay and plaster than to stone. Actually, plaster is a gypsum cement and differs from this group only in being much more versatile.

One of the plasters, Hydrostone, is a very hard and strong cement. Mixed by weight in a proportion of 100 parts Hydrostone to 30 parts of water, it becomes a pourable slurry which sets to a hardness and strength six to eight times that of molding plaster. Its dry density is 110 pounds per cubic foot and its absorption only 23.5 percent of its weight. Otherwise it is very similar to molding plaster. As pointed out more than once before, the less water used in a mix the stronger the set plaster will be. Hydrostone has the property of requiring a smaller amount of water for workability than the other plasters, resulting in its greater strength and density. Its compressive strength increases from 4000 pounds per square inch immediately after setting to 11,000 pounds per square inch when dry, making it preferable to trim or carve on the cast while it is wet. In most plasters there is a five- to ten-minute lag between the time the plaster hardens and the development of its heat of crystallization. This period is somewhat less in Hydrostone and makes it a difficult material to handle in gelatin molds.

Keene's cement, anhydrous calcined gypsum, is a white, comparatively coarse-grained cement which sets in from one to four hours, depending on the grade. It is made by driving off all the water from gypsum in the calcining process and adding accelerators to speed up the setting. When mixed with the minimum amount of water for workability, it sets to a very hard, stone-like mass, being quite dense because its anhydrous condition allows less free water when set. This cement is particularly adaptable to building up on an armature because after starting to set it can be remixed and made plastic again with a small amount of water without loss of strength or hardness. However, this should be done only when the cement is passing from its plastic stage and not after it becomes brittle.

Portland cement is very finely ground calcined hydraulic calcium silicate with a small amount of gypsum added to control the setting when mixed with water. It ranges in color from white to gray and weighs about 100 pounds per cubic foot. It is called a hydraulic cement because, unlike plaster, moisture not only does not affect its setting but aids in its curing. The setting time, from ten to twenty-four hours, can be speeded up by adding calcium chloride to the mixture. Complete curing and maximum strength are reached in twenty-eight days. It is used extensively in building and road construction and is excellent for large sculptures which are to be placed out-of-doors.

Magnesia cements are made by mixing magnesium oxide with magnesium chloride or magnesium sulfate (Epsom salts). The oxide is a fine white powder; the chloride and sulfate are obtained in crystals and must be added to the mixing water in precise proportions. Setting time ranges from four to six hours and can be accelerated by placing the mixture in a dry atmosphere at 100° F to 110° F. It develops a very high strength, considerably greater than Portland cement, but has less resistance to weathering. It takes a high polish when rubbed. This cement is also known as magnesite, and that made with the chloride-water solution, which is best for sculptural purposes, is sometimes called magnesium oxychloride cement.

Concrete and Mortar Mixtures

The name *neat cement* is applied to cement mixed with water only, or in the case of the oxychloride cement, with magnesium chloride and water. When the cement is used as a binder for fillers or aggregates, such as sand, marble chips, gravel and crushed terra cotta or grog, the mixture is called a concrete. Sometimes, only a fine aggregate, such as sand or marble dust, is used; this is called a mortar.

For Portland cement concrete, the aggregates may be any chemically inert substances, but some selection is necessary for oxychloride and Keene's cements, as we shall see later. The properties of the concrete

218

mixture are controlled to a large extent by the aggregates, the cement acting only as a binder to hold the particles together. For instance, Perlite, the trade name of a material made from volcanic rock which weighs from 7 to 12 pounds per cubic foot, can be used to make a very light concrete. One part Portland cement to 5 parts Perlite mixed with 1½ parts of water, by volume, will produce a mass weighing only 30 pounds per cubic foot when dry. This is lighter than most wood and less than half the weight of regular plaster.

The usual concrete mixture for casting is 1 part Portland cement to 3 parts of aggregate. The aggregate is composed of equal parts of fine, medium, and coarse particles. A good test for the proper grading of the aggregate is to mix a sample of known quantities of the dry particles with the right amount of dry cement. Put this in a transparent container, such as a water glass, and see if there is sufficient fine aggregate to fill the spaces between the larger particles. If not, the proportion should be altered to attain a compact mass by the use of less coarse and more fine aggregate. Figure 218 shows four samples of Portland concrete made with various types of aggregates.

Keene's cement, which is not a hydraulic cement, can be cast neat or made into a mortar. The aggregate should not be made up of large, hard particles that might be torn from the cast in working over the surface, or a substance that retains moisture for long periods. Talc, marble dust, Perlite, or pumice can be used but should not exceed in volume the amount of cement used in the mixture. Neat Keene's cement is slightly stronger than this mortar, but in many cases the textural quality of the mortar warrants the loss in strength.

Aggregates for magnesium oxychloride mixtures must be dry when mixed because any uncombined moisture in them will weaken the cement. This material sets hard enough so that there is little danger of hard aggregate being torn out in filing or carving over the surface. The one exception may be large pieces of flint. An excellent aggregate can be made by crushing scraps of different colors from previous castings or by especially preparing sheets of colored magnesite, which are pulverized as soon as they have set. Another is a mixture of equal parts of marble dust, medium grog, and white marble chips. In addition to the colored aggregates, dry pigments can be added to the mixture. Strong concentrates of earth pigments, such as umbers, ochers, and siennas, are least likely to weaken the structure of the concrete because they will not affect the cement chemically and smaller amounts are necessary. A brand of dry pigment known as Mapico is strong enough so that any desired intensity can be made within the maximum limit of 10 percent by volume. If pigments are used, they should be mixed with the dry ingredients as part of the aggregate.

Casting with Concrete

Concrete can be cast in any of the molds previously discussed. Plaster molds should be thoroughly sealed by giving the inner surface two coats of shellac or lacquer followed by a continuous film of grease or heavy oil. Any absorption of the mixing water before complete hardening of the cement will result in cracks in the cast. Flexible molds are preferable to plaster molds because, with the exception of gelatin, there is no problem of absorption. If a gelatin mold is used, its surface should be sealed with a coating of grease since it will not only draw moisture from the cast but will swell and distort in the process.

The dry ingredients of the concrete should be mixed together thoroughly and wetted by pouring the water over them while stirring constantly. A minimum amount of water should be used to make a workable mix, ranging from a stiff paste to a thick liquid.

Magnesium oxychloride mixtures are made by gauging magnesium oxide with a solution of water and magnesium chloride. The concentration of this solution must be accurately measured with a Baumé hydrometer; the proper strength is indicated when the hydrometer reading is 22°. An approximation of this concentration can be made by mixing equal parts by weight of water and magnesium chloride crystals. This should be tested with the hydrometer and more crystals should be added if the reading is below 22°; if the reading is above 22°, additional water should be added. Magnesium sulfate (Epsom salts) added to the solution up to 10 percent, by weight, of the chloride crystals will inactivate any active lime in the mix. When this is done the Baumé reading should be increased to 24°. If the mix is to be stiff —that is, when a smaller amount of the chloride solution is used—the Baumé reading has to be increased to attain the proper weight ratio of 8 to 9 parts of magnesium chloride to 10 parts of magnesium oxide.

When the concrete mix is poured into the mold it should first be puddled with a blunt end stick to insure complete filling, and, if possible, the mold should be vibrated to further release trapped air.

The poured concrete, particularly the slow-setting hydraulic mixtures made with natural or Portland cements, should be covered with damp cloths to prevent evaporation, and, if cast in a plaster mold, the plaster should be saturated with water periodically. These mixtures will set in from ten to twenty-four hours, but it is not safe to remove them from waste molds for several days. The addition of a small amount of calcium chloride (about 2 percent) in the mixing water will accelerate the hardening of Portland cement concrete. When a flexible mold is used, the cast should be taken out as soon as it can stand the strain of removing and should then be covered with damp cloths until cured.

Keene's cement sets faster than Portland cement and, not being a hydraulic material, should not be kept damp while curing. It is necessary, however, to prevent excessive loss of the mixing water by absorption and evaporation before the initial setting occurs.

All concrete casts have a scum on the surface, formed by the extremely fine particles of cement covering the aggregate. This must be cleaned off by grinding or carving over the surface, cutting deep enough to remove the rough surface of the aggregate in order to expose the true color and texture of the aggregate.

Cellular Concrete

An intriguing new building material, called Thermo-con, is prepared with Portland cement, water, and a chemical of mineral origin. Mixed in a special patented generator without aggregate, it increases in volume 125 percent within twenty minutes after being poured and sets in four hours. The finished material is composed of countless very small and uniformly sized hollow spherical cells. These are caused by the action of the chemical on the excess water in the mixture, breaking it down into gases which expand and form an "air aggregate." The material reaches full strength in twenty-eight days and has a density of 45 pounds per cubic foot, about one third that of ordinary concrete. During the setting period some of the gas can be worked out by puddling, producing a denser and stronger cast, when desired. In setting, Thermo-con builds up considerable heat and cannot be cast in a gelatin mold.

In sculpture, Thermo-con can best be used for large castings or those in which the cellular texture does not interfere with the form. Considerably more experimentation is necessary before completely satisfactory casting techniques are developed. For instance, its property of expanding more than twice its poured volume may be eventually utilized to produce a kind of pressure casting by pouring the mold half full and using weights on the openings to restrict the expansion.

Designing for Cast Stone

In sculpture, as in architecture, the concept of concrete as a quick and easy way to produce a stone form can only result in a weak imitation, seldom convincing to anyone. We must conceive of the material as a substance whose properties are controlled by us—that is, we make the material, adding aggregates, color, and strength through re-

219

inforcements to suit our purposes. Its expressive possibilities tend toward expansiveness rather than the restrictions of a given block.

Steel-reinforced concrete should express to some extent the nature of steel, whether or not the steel is actually seen in the form. A light-weight material should be shaped to a visual light-weightedness, and tensile and compressive strengths expressed through appropriate proportions. This does not mean that heavy forms are inappropriate to cast stone; it means that the disposition of weight in the design should follow the indications of this material and technique rather than those of carved stone.

There is no argument against reproducing a stone carving in a concrete mixture similar to the original stone unless one pays homage to the false god of uniqueness. In this case, the cast, if it is a good one, is a stone carving—not a cast-stone design. Similarly, a carving in clay cast in a hard concrete does not become a stone carving, but remains simply a clay carving reproduced in a hard material.

Blocks of concrete with "built-in" properties of hardness, color, and texture can be cast and carved, in which case the form does become that of carved stone. Its character is controlled by the nature of the block of material to the same extent as in carving any other kind of stone. Such blocks should be made with a consistent hardness, equalizing as near as possible the strength of the cement and the aggregate. Blocks of Thermo-con are excellent for carving, especially if the material is made relatively dense and hard. The head in Figure 219 was carved from Thermo-con. The beard and hair were rubbed with white Keene's cement, mixed very stiff, which filled the small hollow cells in those areas.

A Procedure for Cast Stone

A good technique for working with cast stone is to overbuild the model, cast it, and carve it down to the final form. The overbuilding should be more than an extra layer of material to be carved off; it should make allowance for changes in the quality of form as well as texture. This technique allows the maximum expressive function of the material, including its building-up, reinforcing, and carving potentialities.

Figures 220-223 show the development of a design for reinforced magnesium oxychloride concrete. In Figure 220 the sketch shows how the concept of the concrete has been freed of carved-block restriction by making use of a metal framework to reach out into space. The structure of the design is expressed in the stainless steel armature in the same way that structural steel expresses the structure of a building. The joints of the steel framework are silver brazed (Figure 221), using an air-gas torch. Some modifications of the design occur in this stage, partly from the increased size, but mostly in the translation of the aluminum wire framework of the sketch into the steel of the final form.

The concrete form is modeled in clay, and since the shapes are so simple, in this case, they are overbuilt only enough to allow sharpening of edges by filing. Individual waste molds are made of each shape (Figure 222) making certain their accurate replacement on the armature when the clay is removed. A very dense plaster mix should be

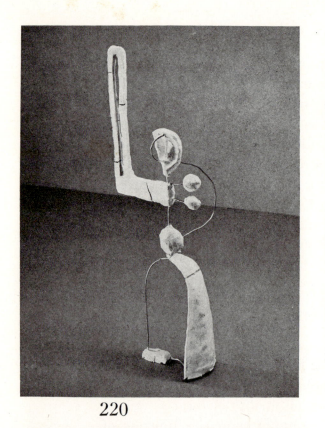

220

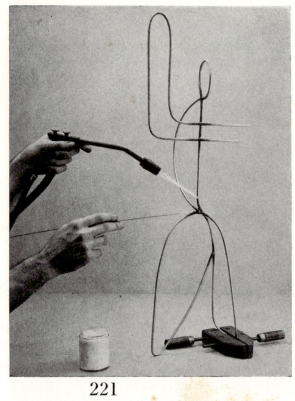

221

222

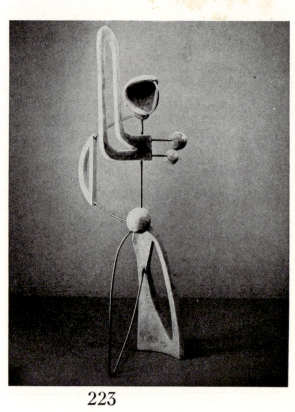

223

used for this kind of mold; a porous mold, even though the surface is sealed, will absorb some of the magnesium chloride solution before the chemical combination is completed, and will result in improper curing.

After the oxychloride concrete has hardened, the molds are removed carefully, avoiding excessive vibration of the steel which might weaken the structure. The completed form (Figure 223) has been filed with a rasp where necessary and the stainless steel polished.

Direct Building in Cement and Concrete

Building up with cement mixtures is similar to direct building in plaster, except that the process is slower and not suitable for small forms. The advantages over plaster, however, are obvious: cement is harder, stronger and more durable; concrete has possibilities of color and texture not possible in plaster; and, particularly with Keene's cement, there is more freedom of surface modeling.

As in the cast magnesite problem above, much of the strength of the form depends on the structure of the armature, but the character of the concrete form determines what armature strength is necessary. In Figure 224 the soft chicken wire foundation is being transformed into a very strong rigid shell by the addition of plaster-saturated burlap. The tensile strength of the wire and burlap, the compressive strength of the plaster, plus the structural strength of the sphere and cylinder, eliminate the necessity of any steel or wooden support. This form is to be developed in a 50-50 mixture of Keene's cement and Perlite. Plaster is used for a foundation because it sets up quickly, and, if the surface is kept rough, there is a strong bond between it and the Keene's cement. If the piece were being built in a Portland cement mixture, finer mesh wire should be used for the armature foundation, and a coat of 3 parts cement and 1 part lime putty built over this to make the foundation.

The Keene's cement mortar is mixed to a dough-like consistency and modeled on with a steel spatula (Figure 225). The working time with one mix of the mortar is about three hours. It can be kept to right modeling plasticity by the addition of a few drops of water when it

224   225

becomes too stiff. Modeling should always be done over a damp surface; if the mixture loses too much water before setting it will be weakened.

Direct modeling with magnesites is too difficult to be practical. The balance between the amounts of oxide and chloride or sulfate is almost impossible to maintain when building a fresh mixture over one that has set. Wetting the hardened material helps but there is danger of reducing the strength of that being added. If such a project is attempted, you should experiment first to find ways of controlling the setting so that extreme unevenness in hardness does not occur.

Casting in Phenolic Resin

Two of the synthetic materials called plastics are discussed here in terms of their possibilities for casting. These materials, phenolic resin and polyester resin, are thermosetting—that is, they become permanently hard upon the application of heat. Koroseal FMC, discussed

206

in the preceding chapter, is a thermoplastic material, becoming fluid when heated.

Phenolic resin is made from phenol, a by-product of coal, and formaldehyde, to which are added catalysts such as distilled water, caustic soda, and an acid solution. These ingredients are mixed and processed at low temperatures, producing a liquid about the consistency of honey. This is the first phase of the development of the phenolic resin and is the condition in which the material is bought. Casting and curing involves the addition of a hardener and heating to the correct temperature. This is described in the procedure below. It is important to keep in mind that the resin is in the process of hardening when bought and becomes more and more viscous with time or above-normal temperatures. Storage life is about eight weeks at 70° F or below.

The following instructions are specifically for a white phenolic resin known as Marblette Resin Number 69.

If a plaster mold is used, it should be given a coat of shellac and two coats of floor wax. Latex molds require a brushing with the castor oil-alcohol separator. Cold Molding Compound should be coated with beeswax thinned with carbon tetrachloride or a film of floor wax. For Koroseal FMC and Elastomer 105 no separator is needed. Before pouring, the mold should be heated to 150° F and rinsed with alcohol to prevent air pockets on the surface.

A hardener furnished with the resin is added in the proportion of 10 percent by weight and must be stirred in thoroughly, scraping the sides and bottom of the mixing container but preventing air bubbles as far as possible. After stirring the mixture, it is left for at least fifteen minutes to allow entrapped air to rise and escape. At room temperature the mixture will remain liquid for several hours.

The resin is poured in the mold slowly and down one side to prevent splashing. The mold is placed in an oven and cured for from thirty minutes to an hour at 180° F. Overheating should be avoided since it darkens the plastic. Complete curing is indicated by the resin becoming a translucent white. The cast can be cooled under running water and removed from the mold immediately. The surface may be filed and polished with No. 400 waterproof sandpaper.

A Marblette casting, such as that shown in Figure 226, is very hard

226   227

and strong, having textural and color qualities similar to ivory. The material can be colored by mixing aniline dyes with the liquid resin. Fillers or aggregates can be used, but when these are stirred with the resin a considerable amount of air enters the mixture. The solution to this problem is to keep the mixture fluid by withholding the hardener until most of this air has risen to the top.

Casting in Polyester Resin

The transparent polyester resin, like the phenolic resin, is obtained as a liquid and requires a catalyst and carefully controlled heat to cure. It can be cast in the same types of molds with the same separators described in the above procedure, but the mold must not be preheated. The mixing and curing of polyester resins must be handled with more precision than Marblette, and require a clear understanding of the material and its polymerization, or setting into a hard substance. However, it is a simple process to follow, and flawless transparent castings, such as that in Figure 227, can be made by the application of a little judgment to the following instructions. This procedure is specifically for an excellent transparent plastic called Selectron 5026.

When the liquid monomer is mixed with the catalyst, Uniperox 60 or butyl hydroperoxide (which is furnished with the resin), it polymerizes first into a gelled state, followed immediately, and in some cases almost simultaneously, by further polymerization into the final thermoset material. During this process the resin undergoes a gradual shrinkage, and, being exothermic, heat is liberated. In thin sections where considerable area is exposed in relation to the total volume, this heat is dissipated quite rapidly and the temperature inside the cast does not rise excessively. However, if the volume is large compared to the surface area, as in a cube or sphere, the heat builds up and internal temperatures of 500° F may be reached. It is obvious that such a temperature differential between the inside and the surface will cause great strains, and cracking is likely to result.

In polymerizing a certain weight of resin, a definite amount of heat is liberated and, as the total amount of heat cannot be controlled, it is necessary to control the rate of heat evolution by varying the amount of catalyst added to the resin. This amount should range from 0.5 percent for thin castings to 0.1 percent for castings one inch or more in thickness. If, as is often the case, a casting has both thick and thin sections the amount of catalyst should be judged in terms of the thickest portion.

The first stage of curing is a process of mildly exothermic gelling, which occurs at room temperature and requires from one half to six hours, depending on the size of the cast and the amount of catalyst employed. In the process of gelling, the catalyst starts decomposing and begins the polymerization of the resin. This occurs slowly at normal temperatures but may be speeded up by a higher temperature or by adding a third ingredient to the mix, a promoter called Selectron 5907. However, this step should be taken only in casting small, thin forms; as the size and thickness of the casting increases, more time is needed to dissipate the heat built up by polymerization.

When the resin becomes gelled, part of the curing process has occurred. The degree of cure which is obtained by room temperature gelation is entirely proportional to the size and shape of the cast. In some cases, when excess catalyst has been used in a thick piece, the cast will be completely cured by the exothermic reaction, but this almost invariably results in strains and cracks in the cured resin. It is best to use the proper amount of catalyst, allow plenty of time for gelation, and then complete the curing by a brief afterbake.

Maximum physical strength properties are obtained by heating the gelled resin at 250° F for five minutes, but since the resin is a poor conductor of heat, actual oven time will be longer. The cured resin will be clearer if the final curing is carried out immediately after gelation. Long delays at this point may produce a slight turbidity in the finished piece. For a casting less than one inch in thickness, thirty minutes at 170° F followed by thirty minutes at 250° F is sufficient. The time should be increased proportionally to the thickness for larger pieces. At no time during the curing process, and especially during gelation, should there be sudden fluctuations in temperatures. The casting should be heated and cooled very slowly. Air has a slight inhibiting action on the curing of the resin, resulting in a sticky surface on the exposed bottom or back of the casting. This can be ground off in finishing or prevented by covering the area with cellophane.

In the case of large castings, after gelation the mold can be placed in a water bath and the water and mold heated. This serves a twofold purpose: exothermic heat is dissipated more rapidly since heat conduction is much better in water than in air, and the rate of external heating will necessarily be slower due to the mass of water. Consequently, sudden changes in temperature will be avoided. The mold should not be in contact with the bottom of the water container where it might receive excessive heating and should be weighted down or braced to prevent upsetting when the water begins to boil.

Polyester resins can be colored with dyes or pigments if desired. The use of fillers such as glass or cotton flock, talc, sand flour, or silene up to 50 percent of the volume will absorb some of the internal strains set up during polymerization. However, remember that excessive use of fillers will weaken the structure of the casting. Large aggregate particles can be used also, but an additional source of strain is introduced due to a difference in coefficient of expansion between the resin and the aggregate, and special care must be taken to control temperature fluctuations.

Selectron Resin can be stored for approximately four months at temperatures below 80° F; at 40° F or lower it is stable for longer periods. This resin is photosensitive and, if stored in glass containers exposed to direct sunlight or even diffused light, may thicken in a few days.

16· Lost Wax Casting

METAL CASTING is one of the oldest and most fascinating processes of sculpture. There are two general methods of transferring a form into metal: the lost wax technique, described in this chapter, and sand molding, which is described in the following chapter. Of the two, lost wax is the oldest, having been used thousands of years ago in much the same manner as presented here. It is a method of making a one-piece mold over a wax model, melting the wax out, and filling the mold with molten metal. Sand molding, which is also of ancient origin, only recently became a highly developed technique; it so well suited the spirit of the Industrial Revolution that the process of lost wax casting became a "lost art." Its revival began in the early part of the twentieth century in the field of dentistry. Now it has again become an important technique, replacing sand molding to a large extent in industrial as well as sculptural casting.

This revival of lost wax casting, however, has developed at a tangent to the original method. The "true" or direct technique which can produce only one cast from a model has been replaced by an indirect method by which multiple casts can be made. The difference in the two procedures lies solely in the manner of producing the wax model. In the direct technique the sculptor builds the model directly in wax; while in the indirect method, the sculptor usually makes his model in clay, casts it in plaster, and sends it to a foundry where it is cast in wax by one of the flexible molding procedures. Once the cast is in wax the subsequent procedures are identical.

Direct Building in Wax

The technique of direct building in wax is close to the method of working directly with metal. Sculpturally, the wax is very much like metal, responding to physical forces, such as heat, pressure, torsion, and tension in a similar manner, but having only a fraction of the resistance of metal. Wax sheets and rods can be cast, cut, shaped, and joined in a manner closely approximating the handling of metal. In working with wax, you can imagine that you have greatly increased strength, and that you are manipulating not wax but the actual metal. However, just as the form in wax will be transferred to metal, your feeling for metal must be transferred to the wax, and this feeling of great power over the material not misused. Another concept is that of the molten metal, accumulating tremendous energy from the furnace, enabling it to flow through space. You direct and guide this energy, expressing it in an appropriate form.

Figures 228-231 show some of the possibilities of working directly in wax. Shapes which have been previously planned are cut from a sheet of microcrystalline wax. Beeswax is also suitable but is more expensive. The parts of the design are joined by fusing the wax with a warm soldering iron (Figure 229) and by holding them in place until cool. If necessary, additional wax can be built up at the joint and cooled by running cold water over the warm wax.

If the form is to be modeled, a special wax mixture is necessary; microcrystalline wax and beeswax are not suitable for modeling but may be built up by fusing bits to the basic form with the soldering iron. A good modeling wax can be made with equal parts of beeswax and paraffin, with the addition of one ounce of lead oleate to each pound of wax. This is melted over a water bath, and ammoniated mercury, in amounts of one to two ounces per pound of mixture, is added and stirred in thoroughly. This fine white powder is suspended

228

229

230

231

in the wax and gives it an opacity which is preferable to the usual translucency of waxes. The excess ammoniated mercury will settle to the bottom. By leaving the melted mixture undisturbed for a few minutes and pouring off all but the residue in the bottom of the container, only the suspended particles of ammoniated mercury will be included in the wax. Talc could be used for this purpose and handled in the same way, but it is more apt to continue settling out and often leaves a residue in the mold for the metal cast. Vaseline added in amounts up to 25 percent will adjust the hardness for modeling in cold weather. The cream color of this mixture can be changed by the addition of a small amount of an oil-soluble aniline dye such as a photographic tinting color. When all the ingredients are thoroughly mixed, the wax is left in its molten state ten or fifteen minutes to allow any unsuspended solids to settle out. It is then poured on wet plaster or wood boards to cool. The initial set will be somewhat hard and stiff but working it between the fingers will make it very plastic. A simpler modeling wax can be made by softening microcrystalline wax with vaseline or Venice turpentine, but it lacks the quality of the above mixture.

The wax structure may need some extra support in warm weather. Braces made of wax rods attached at strategic points with the soldering iron will serve this purpose (Figure 230). Plaster spatulas work well as modeling tools but should be kept clean by wiping them periodically with a cloth dampened with carbon tetrachloride. A form may also be developed by bending, twisting, and joining flat sheet-like shapes as shown in Figure 231, and by resorting to modeling only when more thickness or a different texture is needed.

For a hollow cast, a core must be constructed first, and wax which will determine the thickness and surface of the metal is built over it. This core is an "inside mold" and is usually removed from the metal cast leaving a hollow area inside the cast the shape of the core.

An armature of aluminum or brass wire is constructed for a form requiring reinforcement (Figure 232). Over this any of the molding compositions used for metal casting (which are discussed later) is built up to within ¼ inch of the final surface (Figure 233). The material used here is a commercial product, called Non-Ferrous Investment

232

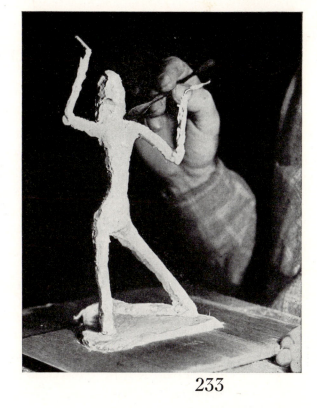

233

234

235

Number 1, and is a mixture of plaster and highly refractory substances such as talc. It is mixed very much like ordinary plaster, using more water than in a regular mix, and sets in about the same time, though with less hardness.

Wax is modeled on the core (Figure 234), or in some cases, it may be built up by cutting strips of wax from a sheet and laying them edge to edge over the core. In both methods the final thickness of the wax, which will be the thickness of the metal, should be about ¼ inch, not varying from this more than $\frac{1}{16}$ inch. The completed wax model (Figure 235) is next prepared for casting as described later.

The Cast Wax Model

Returning to casting, we will consider the problems of making a cast wax model as used in the indirect method of lost wax casting.

A Cold Molding Compound mold requires no separator for wax; neither do Koroseal FMC or Elastomer 105 molds. Latex should be brushed with kerosene. Gelatin, which is usually used in foundries, requires a coating of the stearin-kerosene separator, and, owing to its low melting point, the method of filling it with hot wax will be given special consideration later. A plaster piece mold needs no separator other than complete saturation with water.

There are two methods of casting wax in a mold: pouring and brushing. These correspond roughly to the two techniques of casting plaster in a waste mold or to those of casting clay in a piece mold.

For pouring the mold, in this case, the poured CMC mold made in Chapter 14 is assembled and tied or clamped firmly (Figure 236). Microcrystalline wax, having a melting point between 160° F and 180° F, is melted in a double boiler or roaster oven. The assembly shown in Figure 237 is ideal for this purpose. Top heat is controlled by raising or lowering the radiant broiler for moderate or rapid melting, and the oven temperature control is set at the pouring temperature. When the wax is melted, the broiler is removed and the oven covered for a few minutes until the heat equalizes at the oven temperature.

The pouring temperature will vary with the melting point of a specific wax; and it must be remembered that this melting point will

236

237

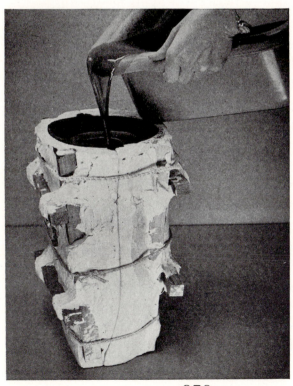

238

239

increase with repeated or continued heating, as some of the more volatile substances are driven from the wax. The only rule is to pour the wax at the lowest temperature at which it takes a good impression, which is usually from five to ten degrees over the melting point. Wax poured at too low a temperature will trap air between the wax and surface of the mold, causing a poor impression, air holes, and lap lines. Wax that is too hot will stick to the mold. Carnauba wax added in amounts from 5 to 10 percent will increase the melting point but will cause the wax to take a better impression at a temperature closer to the melting point. This, of course, results in less shrinkage in the cast. A small amount of vaseline added to the wax will reduce the melting point. There is no contradiction in the addition of both carnauba wax and vaseline since the carnauba wax helps produce a sharp surface to the cast regardless of the melting point.

The melted wax is poured into the mold rapidly but without splashing (Figure 238), filling it to the level of the bottom. Almost immediately, the cool mold becomes coated with a thin layer of solidified wax, and if the molten wax is poured out, a thin coating is left on the mold. However, the sudden chilling of the wax is apt to trap air between this coating and the mold. If the hot wax is left in the mold two or three minutes, the mold itself will begin to get warm and part of the chilled layer of wax will be remelted. This allows some of the air to escape, and avoids lap lines. Small projecting parts of the mold will get hotter than more massive areas, and if the hot wax is left inside too long a layer of wax uneven in thickness will be built up. When the hot wax is poured back into the roaster pan, it is poured slowly and the mold rotated to cause the wax to flow over the entire surface (Figure 239). The pan is replaced in the roaster to retain its heat, and the mold with its thin coating of wax is left to cool to room temperature. Running cold water inside the mold or blowing with compressed air will speed up the cooling. If water is used, care should be taken to see that none is left inside.

A second layer of wax is deposited by repeating this process. The wax in the roaster will be slightly cooler for this second pouring and can be left inside the mold for four or five minutes. Wherever possible, projections inside the mold should be given an additional coating of wax by brushing, since the wax is almost invariably thinner in these areas. A third pouring is usually sufficient to build up the required thickness of ¼ inch, and the hollow cast is left inside the mold until cool and hard.

One of the problems in the above method is the control of the heating up of the mold. Unless you are very cautious, the portion of the mold that contains the hot wax the longest will become hotter and have a thinner area of wax formed on it. A variation on this technique that helps to avoid heating the mold is to fill the mold partially, one third to one half full, and to immediately flow the wax over the entire surface, picking up the mold, tilting it, and rolling the wax around the inside and out the opening back into the pan. The temperature of the wax can be a little higher when using this method.

Small or thin pieces present no problems since there is not enough heat in the wax to cause sticking. If less than ¾ inch in thickness, the cast can be solid, in which case the mold is simply filled and left to cool.

For the brushing technique, a resin-wax mixture is easier to handle than wax alone. The resin cools more slowly and helps avoid brush marks and lap lines. The following is a method of preparing a simple resin-wax mixture:

1. Use a weight proportion of one part microcrystalline wax to three parts pulverized rosin, an inexpensive resin.

2. Melt the wax completely and stir in the rosin, being careful not to exceed 200° F, which would prevent the rosin from mixing with the wax.

3. Turn off the heat as soon as the wax and rosin begin to mix, allowing the built-up heat to complete the fusion. Too much heat oxidizes the rosin and causes it to separate. It also raises the melting point.

4. Small amounts (up to 5 percent) of carnauba wax and vaseline may be added to increase the flowing quality and lower the melting point. These should be melted with the microcrystalline wax before adding the rosin.

5. If there is trouble in mixing the rosin with the wax, increase the amount of rosin. It mixes best when at least three quarters of the mixture is rosin.

The melting point of the resin-wax mixture should be low enough to prevent quick chilling; the actual temperature, of course, depends on the room temperature. It is best to start at one edge of the mold and flow the wax with the brush loaded with melted wax. Avoid adding hot wax to an area that has hardened since this is apt to result in lap lines. A test piece can be made by covering part of the mold, removing it when cool, and inspecting the surface. If brush marks show, the wax is not hot enough; if lap lines show the melting point may be too high and more vaseline should be added.

A coat ⅛ inch or less in thickness is built up, except on projections and ridges of the mold, which should be about ¼ inch. When the mold is eventually filled, these areas will become warmer than the rest of the mold and will increase little if any in thickness. The edges of the wax coating are beveled to allow wax to seal the joint, just as the plaster coating in a waste mold is prepared for fresh plaster to run between the sections (page 155).

The mold is bound together and filled with the resin-wax mixture, just sufficiently hot to flow easily. If the mixture is too hot, it will melt the wax inside the mold instead of building up the thickness of the cast. A good test is to insert into the hot wax a piece of the cooled mixture about the same thickness as the coating, leaving it there for a minute. If part of it is melted away, the wax is too hot, but if a thin coating is added it is about right. The final thickness of the cast can usually be reached by leaving the liquid wax in the mold two or three minutes.

The mixture of microcrystalline wax suggested for pouring can also be used for brushing, though it is more difficult to avoid brush marks and lap lines. It is preferable to the resin mixture, however, in cases where you are particularly concerned with surface texture. The wax-resin composition leaves a residue in the mold for metal which is made from the wax cast. If the microcrystalline mixture is used, the melting point may have to be lowered by adding vaseline in order to get a good impression of the mold's surface. Since the rate of cooling depends on room temperature and the particular grade of wax, the only way the necessary amount of vaseline can be decided upon is by tests such as those mentioned in preceding paragraphs. Generally, for a

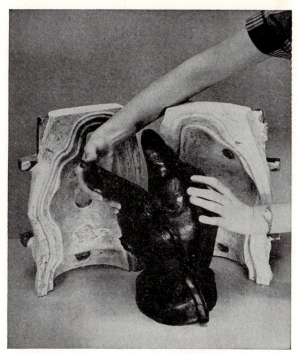

240   241

room temperature of 70° F and a wax melting at 140° F, 5 percent vaseline (melting point 115° F) is ample. As you become more experienced with the technique of brushing, you may reduce the vaseline or eliminate it entirely.

It may be advisable at times to pour the plaster composition core inside the wax cast before removing the mold. This will be the case if the cast is made with a low-melting wax mixture during warm weather, or if the structure of the form seems to need the core for support. The cast being removed from the mold in Figure 240 is still hollow, and the core will be poured later.

There are several ways of handling the problem of casting wax in gelatin molds. The simplest and perhaps the most satisfactory is the brushing technique. Wax applied in this manner cools quickly and will not build up enough heat in the gelatin to melt the surface. A good system is to use a low-melting-point wax for the first thin coating and then to brush over that with a harder wax. When joining the brushed-on sections, it is quite important to prevent the wax that is poured into the mold from building up heat in the gelatin. A good idea is to pour the wax down one seam until the mold is about one quarter filled and then pour it out the other. If more thickness is needed in other areas, the mold can be rolled to deposit additional wax. At no time should the mold be filled with hot wax and allowed to stand for a period of time. Another method is to assemble the mold and pour in a small amount of low-melting wax, rolling the mold quickly to deposit an even layer over the surface. The excess is poured out and the mold allowed to cool completely. Then additional thickness is built up by pouring in small amounts of resin-wax and rolling it over the first layer.

The Lost Wax Mold

The first step in making a lost wax mold is gating or channeling the metal through the mold and into the cavity which will be left by the melted-out wax. There are several general systems, but each piece becomes a unique problem. The gating system shown partially in Figure 241 is more usual and safer than those that follow, but not necessarily the best. When it is melted out, the large rod of wax will make the main channel through which the metal will flow; and the smaller gates branching off and joining the cast will allow the metal to enter the cast. Where they join the cast they need not be more than ¼ inch in diameter for a casting of this size. We can see just how they function by referring to Figure 252 (page 230), which shows the total gating system in pouring position. The gates angle up from the main channel so that the metal enters the cast without agitation. In other words, it enters the cast only when the level of the molten metal is at that point and does not fall through the portion of the mold that makes the cast.

There are both advantages and disadvantages to this system of gating. There is a smoother flow of metal into the cast area, less danger of breaking projections in the mold, and faster filling of the mold which prevents chilling of the metal. The disadvantages are the difficulty of removing the numerous gates and reworking the surface where they were attached, and the large amount of metal necessary to fill the mold. Other systems of gating are discussed at the end of this section.

242   243

When this portion of the gating is completed, small nails are pushed
through the wax and left projecting both inside and out to anchor the
core to the mold when the wax is removed.   Only three or four are
needed in a small model such as this.   Next, a mold is built up around
the wax with a plaster composition.   The commercial project, Non-
Ferrous Investment Number 1, mentioned earlier, is satisfactory for
the first initial coating.   Another composition that is suitable for this
facing coat is two parts of plaster to three parts of silica flour.   Fine
grog, pumice, or talc can be substituted for the silica.   If the plaster-
silica mixture is used, the two should be combined before mixing with
water.   Either composition should be mixed like regular plaster but
a little on the light rather than the heavy side.   The mold surface
should be hard enough to withstand the force of the metal but porous

244

245

246

247

enough to absorb some of the gases which are inevitable in molten metal.

Brushing or spraying the wax with alcohol immediately before applying the facing coat will help prevent air bubbles on its surface. The investment mixture, in this case NFI No. 1, should be brushed on carefully and systematically, starting from the bottom (Figure 242). The facing coat should be between ¼ and ½ inch thick and should cover the entire wax structure. Subsequent layers will not come in contact with the metal and serve primarily as a support for the facing. These can be made with coarser and cheaper materials. Luto, molds for metal which have been used and pulverized, can be added to either the NFI or the plaster-silica in amounts up to half the total mixture. A good proportion is two parts plaster, three parts silica, and three parts luto, or two parts NFI to three parts luto—by volume.

As the building-up continues, the investment can be applied more freely (Figure 243), but large air pockets should be avoided. Wrapping the mold with soft iron wire as shown in Figure 244 will help prevent cracking, and in some molds, metal supports may be necessary for strength. When this part of the mold is completed, the top is flattened so that it will stand upside down (Figure 245).

Turned up, the bottom shows the hollow cast and the ends of the wax channel. A core consisting of one of the luto mixtures is poured inside the cast. Small nails are driven part way into the bottom of the core and the mold to insure a strong joint with the final part of the mold. Wax rods are joined to the ends of the channel and brought to a junction where an inverted conical-shaped piece of wax is attached. This will form a funnel when melted out, into which the molten metal will be poured. Several wax rods are attached to the bottom of the cast and the top of this funnel for vent openings for the escape of hot air and gases as the metal rises in the mold (Figure 246).

This structure is covered with a facing coat of investment, followed by the coarser luto mixture (Figure 247). It is also reinforced with wire, wrapped across the joint to help prevent separation. The completed mold (Figure 248) is trimmed up and is ready for removal of the wax.

Calcining the Mold

Before molten metal can be poured into the mold, not only must the wax be melted out but the investment material must be heated to a temperature of about 500° F to drive off all free and combined moisture and any gases left in the mold by the molten wax. This calcining and the removal of the wax can be done in one operation in a kiln by making a metal trough arrangement to carry off the molten wax. All the wax, except that absorbed by the mold, will run out by the time the temperature of the inside of the mold reaches 200° F, provided there are no areas inside the mold that trap the wax. When the wax has drained out of the kiln, the trough can be taken out, the kiln door closed and the temperature carried up to 500° F or more. As a general rule, molds three inches in thickness require from fourteen to sixteen hours at 400°-500° F to dehydrate and calcine. Thicker molds require more time in proportion to their thickness. The time can be decreased by raising the temperature; the mold will withstand temperatures of from 1000°-1500° F. A mold the size of the one illustrated here should be carried to a red heat and held there until all the gases from the wax are burned out. This can be watched through an opening in the kiln since the gases ignite and burn with a blue flame at the funnel and vents. The entire calcining procedure may require from twenty-four to thirty-six hours, because when the heat is turned off, the mold must be left in the kiln until cool enough to handle without gloves.

Another way of removing the wax from the mold is to place it over boiling water. A large metal container such as a garbage can is used. The mold is placed on several bricks, funnel end down, and water poured into the container up to the top of the bricks but not covering any part of the mold. The top may be covered with a piece of oilcloth to help retain the heat. Several hours of steaming will melt the wax and leave it deposited on top of the water. It can be reclaimed for further use by trimming off the lower portion containing foreign matter and adding vaseline if necessary to reduce its hardness. After steaming out the wax, the mold is calcined as described above but without having to use a trough to drain the wax from the kiln.

248   249

Pouring the Mold

When the calcining process is completed, all the shapes that were originally in wax are hollow areas inside the mold and it is ready to cast (Fig.
249).   The mold is rather fragile and porous, and should be filled with
metal before it has a chance to absorb moisture from the atmosphere.
To hold the mold steady while pouring the metal and also to strengthen
the investment material, it is placed inside a larger container and the
space around the mold filled with dry sand.

Any nonferrous metal such as lead, aluminum, brass, or bronze can
be cast in this mold.   Lead, which has a low melting point (618° F),
can be melted in small quantities over an ordinary gas burner.   Aluminum, brass, and bronze, which melt at about 1220°, 1630° and
1830° F respectively, must be melted in a furnace.   There are many
types and sizes of furnaces.   A gas-fired furnace equipped with an air
blower and capable of melting fifty or sixty pounds of bronze is practical for small castings such as that demonstrated here.   The metal is
heated in a graphite or silicon carbide container called a crucible.

227

Bronze and brass are both alloys of copper. Number 1 bronze, or red brass as it is usually called, contains 85 percent copper, 5 percent tin, 5 percent zinc, and 5 percent lead. It is a good casting metal, has a rich, warm color, and responds readily to surface working. Generally, when a copper alloy contains over 3 percent tin and less than 12 percent zinc it is called tin bronze or red brass. Aluminum bronze is made by adding about 10 percent aluminum to copper. It is a hard, corrosion-resistant, golden-yellow material, but more difficult to cast than tin bronze. Yellow brass contains from 15 percent to 38 percent zinc. It casts well and takes a very high polish.

It is much more practical to buy the alloyed metal from a foundry or smelter than to attempt mixtures of small amounts of metal. It is also bad practice to mix scrap metal of unknown composition with ingot metal; blends of the above alloys seldom produce a good metal. Of all the possible combinations, there are only twenty-seven specifications used in commercial casting. While the alloy is being heated it undergoes a slight change in composition. There are small losses through volatilization of zinc, tin, and lead. Ingot specifications are designed to allow for this change in composition under ordinary melting conditions. However, when remelting former castings, the small amount of low-melting metal that volatilized can be replaced. This is necessarily a matter of guesswork, but common practice is to add one ounce of zinc to 100 pounds of molten yellow brass, just before pouring. In a similar manner, equal amounts of tin, zinc, and lead, totaling about one ounce per 100 pounds of metal, are added to red brass. The volatilization of these metals can be reduced by putting a flux, such as glass, in the crucible with the cold metal. This forms a crust on top of the molten metal and also picks up any slag and foreign matter. It is skimmed off just before pouring.

The metal should be heated well beyond its melting point, which is the temperature at which it begins to melt. There is a lag in the rise of the temperature between the time the first crystal melts (solidus point) and the instant the metal is completely molten (liquidus point). In other words, a certain amount of heat is used for the physical change from solid to liquid without increasing the temperature of the metal. The interval in heat between solidus and liquidus is called the solidification range and is about 200° F in copper-base alloys. It is

228

250

during this period that most of the metal's expansion takes place (from 4.5 percent to 9 percent). Once the metal is completely liquid, its temperature can be increased by continuing the heat input. The casting temperature should be about 200° F above the melting point, and to allow for cooling while skimming and preparing to pour, the metal is superheated another 100° F. Yellow brass should be brought to about 1950° F and red brass to about 2150° F.

Experienced foundrymen judge the temperature of metal by its color and reaction in the crucible. A pyrometer which can measure to at least 2500° F should be used unless one has great confidence in his ability to judge the metal by eye.

When the correct temperature has been reached the furnace is turned off and the slag skimmed from the top of the metal. The crucible is removed from the furnace by lifting it with specially designed tongs that fit snugly around its sides, and is placed inside the ring of the pouring shank. About .02 percent of phosphorus (2 ounces of 15-percent phosphor-copper per 100 pounds of metal) is added to make the metal more fluid.

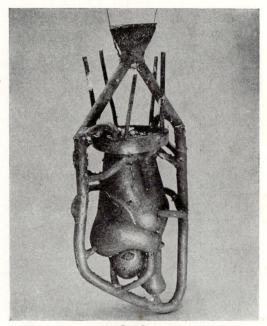

251   252

When the temperature drops to the pouring point, the crucible is lifted by the shank and the metal poured steadily into the mold (Figure 250). Here the alloy being poured is yellow brass. The white smoke, characteristic of molten yellow brass, is vapor from the oxidizing zinc. Two ounces of aluminum added to 100 pounds of yellow brass will eliminate most of this smoke; aluminum has a higher affinity than zinc for oxygen, and when present in the melt is preferentially oxidized, forming nonvolatile aluminum oxide. Its presence also increases the fluidity of the alloy.

Removing the Cast

The mold should not be opened until the cast has cooled; unlike steel or wrought iron, brass and bronze are very brittle at temperatures around 1000° F and a sharp blow could break a large section. Cracking may occur also from uneven shrinkage if some parts are cooled more rapidly than others. The investment is broken away (Figure 251) with a small hammer or pick, and the broken mold is saved for making luto. The entire former wax structure, now in yellow brass, is shown in Figure 252.

Metal castings of this kind are rarely perfect. Small cracks inside the mold produce thin projections of metal called fins, such as that on the leg in Figure 252. These can result from uneven shrinkage of the investment material in calcining, sudden chilling of the calcined mold, or insufficient strength of the mold. These are not serious, but they do require some reworking of the surface. Blow-holes or spongy surfaces often occur when the mold has been improperly calcined or has picked up moisture, though the most common reason for them is excessive gases in the metal and lack of permeability of the investment. Venting cannot release these gases since most of them separate from the metal while it is changing from a liquid to a solid and the metal in the vents, unless they are very large, becomes solid before that in the cast. Spongy surfaces may also result from shrinkage due to improper gating. Just as there is expansion when the metal melts, there is shrinkage during solidification. As a rule, gates should be placed on the thickest sections of the cast since the metal in those areas solidifies last. The principle involved here is that molten metal will be fed through these thicker sections to counteract shrinkage in the thinner sections.

The most common defects from gases are caused by excessive hydrogen in tin bronzes and carbon dioxide or carbon monoxide in yellow brasses. If the metal in the pouring funnel mushrooms as it cools, there is excessive gas in the metal; if it shrinks and sinks as shown in Figure 251, the gases have been properly eliminated.

The solution to the gas problem in copper-brass alloys is in controlling the oxygen content of the metal. It is essential to melt in an oxidizing atmosphere—that is, adjusting the combustion in the furnace so that there is enough air to prevent drawing oxygen from the metal. A reducing atmosphere or excessive reducing elements in the metal, such as phosphorus, will cause the formation of gases in the cast. If excessive phosphorus is present in the metal it can be eliminated by the addition of an oxidizing agent such as copper oxide. In tin bronzes, the zinc added to adjust melting losses creates a flushing action which helps in getting rid of the dissolved hydrogen, and the addition of .02 percent phosphor-copper just before pouring helps maintain the equilibrium of the hydrogen-oxygen reaction. Oxidizing melting alone will prevent excessive carbon absorption in yellow brass, although

231

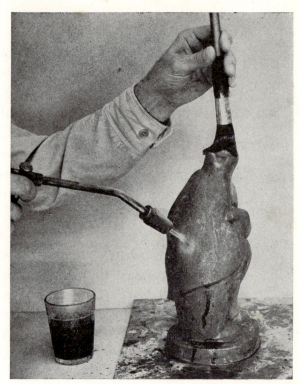

253   254

breaking the crust and allowing the metal to flare for a short period will also help. Aluminum in a copper alloy forms an oxide film on the surface of the molten metal. Periodically breaking this crust and agitating gently by working the rod up and down allows the absorbed hydrogen to escape.

Chasing and Coloring

The gating structure is cut off the cast with a hack saw leaving a slight projection where the gates entered the cast. These are removed carefully with cold chisels or pneumatic metal chippers (Figure 253). The metal should be cleaned by dipping it in a pickling solution of one part sulfuric acid to 100 parts water to remove all oxidized metal and particles of investment; it should then be thoroughly washed with water. The core, which becomes quite soft when wet, is dug out.

The process of finishing the metal surface is called chasing. It often involves the plugging of holes such as those made by the anchor nails in the core. This is done by drilling the hole to a standard size, threading it, and screwing in a plug made of metal identical with the cast. The surface texture is made consistent by the use of files and punches. Some accenting and reworking of surface is usually desirable to bring more life into the metal.

If left alone, metal will in time acquire its own color or patina. Acid solutions and heat applied to the metal hasten the natural process of oxidation. To do this well requires the same restraint and respect for the material as staining wood. Heavy crusty patinas should be used only on pieces designed for that particular effect, just as a glaze should not be put arbitrarily on a terra cotta. As a rule, metal that is polished or thinly patinaed is more expressive of metal than those heavily coated.

Coloring metal with acids and heat is largely a matter of experimentation, since there are so many variables in the composition of the metal and the manner of application. Cast metal has a skin, a thin layer of metal that is chill-hardened by the surface of the mold. In some cases, silicon from the mold alloys with the surface metal and increases this hardness. This skin resists oxidation and makes pieces with a cast texture more difficult to color than those in which the surface is filed down. The following suggestions are necessarily generalized.

Copper oxidizes more readily than its usual alloys. If a piece is to be colored, it should be cast in a tin bronze; if it is to be polished, in a yellow brass. Bronze can be polished but it will not hold its luster; yellow brass can be colored but not so easily as bronze.

Copper nitrate or copper sulfate will produce a green film when dissolved in 10 parts of water and brushed on hot bronze. Washing immediately and repeating the process several times will build up an even color. Potassium sulfide or iron nitrate mixed to a 1-percent solution with water will make dark browns and blacks if applied to bronze in the same manner. A formula for yellow-green on bronze or brass is: 7 parts ammonium chloride, 4 parts copper acetate, and 8 parts water, by weight. A dark blue-green can be made with 1 part sodium thiosulfate, 8 parts iron nitrate, and 128 parts water.

Bronze and brass can be colored by heat alone. A few experiments on scraps, carrying the metal to varying heat colors and cooling suddenly or slowly, will illustrate many possibilities. Also a reducing

255

256

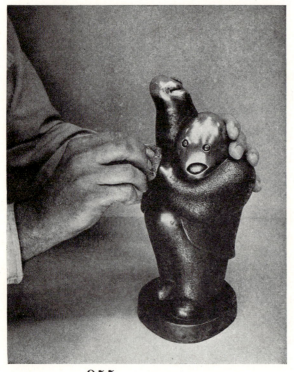

257

258

flame played over an oxidized surface or one coated with a film of copper oxide will produce interesting effects. In heating bronze or brass, it should be remembered that they lose malleability as the temperature is raised to a red heat, and become quite brittle.

Both aluminum and lead can be darkened by muriatic acid. A thin deposit of copper will adhere to lead if copper oxide is mixed with the acid and the surface heated. Tests should be made first to be sure of not melting the lead.

In Figure 254 the yellow brass cast is being patinaed with a solution of potassium sulfide and water. The metal is kept just above 200° F so that the liquid steams when it is applied. Periodically, the cast is washed and dried to observe the color. Polished areas are rubbed with fine steel wool (Figure 255). If they become too bright the application of a little heat will darken and dull them. The finished cast (Figure 256) has been given a light coat of wax to protect the metal from further oxidation.

Two other gating systems, having obvious advantages over the preceding one, are shown in Figures 257 and 258. These casts are in tin bronze, which can be cast with smaller gates and runners than yellow brass. The rods on the upper part of the piece in Figure 257 are air vents and served only to release trapped air as the metal flowed in. The cast was poured upside down—not in the position shown here. Small brass pins were used to anchor the core and were fused with the cast so that it was necessary only to cut them off at the surface. The cast shown in Figure 258 has practically no work to be done on its surface. The core was anchored with pins as in Figure 257, and since all the gates enter the bottom, only two small vents, one on the elbow and one on the head, need chasing.

Figures 259-262 show some of the possibilities of lost wax casting. The bug (Figure 259) illustrates the freedom with which large and thin sections of metal can be handled together in a lost wax mold; it emphasizes the fact that anything that can be made in wax can be cast in metal through this process. The form in Figure 260 shows the directness of approach to metal through wax. Figure 261 illustrates not only a complex casting problem but a concept of unending rhythmical

235

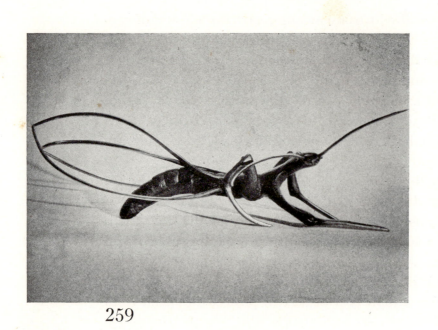

259

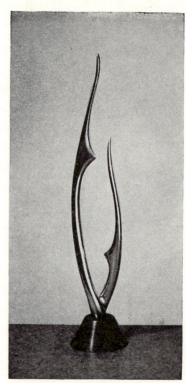

260

261

262

structure expressive of the dynamic nature of metal itself. The surface quality of the form and the rhythmical design in Figure 262 help express the well-founded feeling that the metal flowed into this position and froze there.

It is interesting to note the extent to which bronze sculptures throughout the ages consistently depict the quality of metal form. One sees a marked similarity in the bronzes of nearly all periods. The fluidity of form characteristic of the metal sculptures of ancient Oriental and Occidental cultures persists in those of our own age as typified by some of the works of Rodin, Epstein, and Lipchitz. In many cases there is a closer similarity of form quality among bronzes of widely separated origins, early Greek and Chinese for example, than between a bronze sculpture and a carving of the same culture. Almost invariably, where there is deviation from the bronze form it is obvious that the sculptor was intentionally trying to imitate another material.

Of course, the persistence of form quality can be traced through other sculptural materials. However, it is especially striking in bronzes because the flexibility of this material makes almost any quality of form possible.

17 · Sand Molding and Casting

A SAND MOLD is a piece mold made of fine damp sand pressed and packed around the model. The sand must be of such a quality that it will not fall into pieces when lifted off the model. In simple, two-piece molds, it is rammed into frames of wood or metal placed around the model to help hold the sand together. These frames are called flasks. When molding a complex form, requiring a number of pieces, the sand in the flask acts as a shell, similar to that in the plaster piece mold. In this case the smaller pieces within the shell are made with a composition of sand, flour, and molasses water so that they will be sturdy enough to handle. Cores for hollow casts are made with sharp sand—that is, sand with sharp-edged particles that interlock when pressed together. This sand is usually coarser than molding sand.

Sand molding and casting has two advantages over the lost wax process: the sand is more porous than the plaster composition and allows gases from the metal to escape more readily, and the mold, in most cases, can be made and cast in much less time. On the other hand, the sand process has a number of disadvantages. The sand does not take the fine impression of plaster compositions. The cast is less apt to be accurate and requires more chasing, since a lost wax mold is invariably one piece and a sand mold may require any number of pieces. Complex forms are usually cut into several sections to simplify casting when a sand mold is used. Sand molds can be made only from hard models such as plaster, and this makes it necessary to build directly in plaster or cast in it before making the sand mold.

Generally, small simple pieces which are to be filed down and polished are best cast in sand molds since the metal will have less chance of being spongy and the mold can be made quickly. Also, large castings in which slight inaccuracies of registration and surface are not of great importance may be cast in sand to avoid the problem of calcining a large mold. The one thing that can always be done better in sand than plaster investment is casting in iron and iron alloys. The gypsum in plaster compositions attacks the hot iron and produces a bad surface. The demonstration presented here is for cast iron, but the same procedure could be used for bronze, brass, or aluminum.

Sand Mold Procedure

The plaster model (Figure 263) must be shellacked and then dusted with talc to remove all stickiness. The form is marked off into the necessary sections to avoid undercuts. In this case, one side can be made in one piece and the other in three pieces.

Sand is rammed into one flask which will be the bottom of the mold; this is called the drag. An area is scooped out to fit the simplest side of the model, leaving extra room for freshly sifted or riddled sand into which the model is firmly pressed. Sand is built up and packed against the model, making a clean surface or parting (Figure 264). The model may be lifted at this stage to see that the parting does not include small undercuts. If it is lifted, it should be replaced very carefully to avoid damaging the surface of the mold.

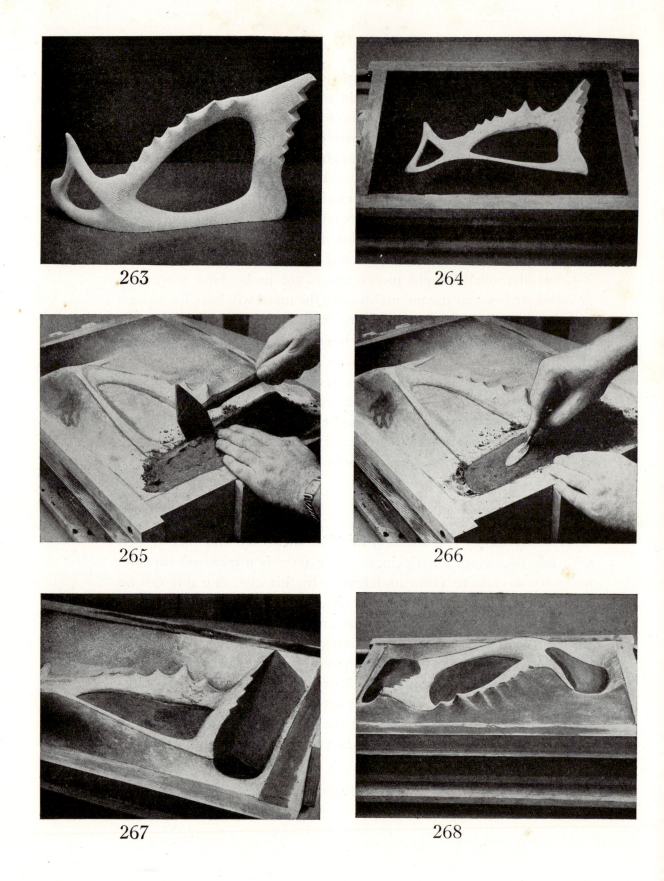

263

264

265

266

267

268

A parting compound of silicon flour or pumice is dusted over the surface of the drag to prevent the subsequent pieces from adhering to it. One of the pieces in the top part of the mold, or cope, is being packed against the model with a wooden mallet in Figure 265. This material is a composition of 1 part flour, 2 parts molasses, and 20 parts sand. It will be strong enough to lift without fracturing after drying for a short time. The piece is further pressed and troweled with a molding tool (Figure 266). The surface is smoothed and the piece trimmed to its proper boundary, being sure there are no undercuts on its surface (Figure 267). The second piece is made in a similar manner (Figure 268). The entire surface is then dusted with an additional parting compound.

The flask for the cope is placed on top of that for the drag, and is registered by wedge-shaped pins on each end (Figure 269). The inside of the flask has grooves to help hold the sand when it is eventually lifted. A heavy coat of clay slip is painted over the wood to prevent absorption of moisture from the sand and also to help grip it to the flask. A ¾-inch rod called a sprue cutter is attached vertically to the drag. This rod will make a channel through the cope for the metal to enter the mold.

Sand is riddled over the drag, model, and pieces until an inch thick. Then, a shovel full of sand is dropped heavily on top of the first layer by a quick motion of the shovel. The force of the falling sand packs the soft riddled layer evenly against the model. This is repeated until the cope flask is about half full. The relatively loose sand is rammed to make it a compact mass, care being taken to direct most of the force toward the sides of the flask where more strength and less permeability is needed. The flask is then filled with sand and rammed tightly (Figure 270). The sprue cutter is removed by tapping it lightly and pulling it through the cope.

The cope is lifted straight up from the drag and put carefully aside (Figure 271). The two small pieces are taken off the model and placed in the cope section. The model can be loosened by tapping on it with a padded wooden mallet and it is then removed from the drag. The mold is now complete except for the core.

241

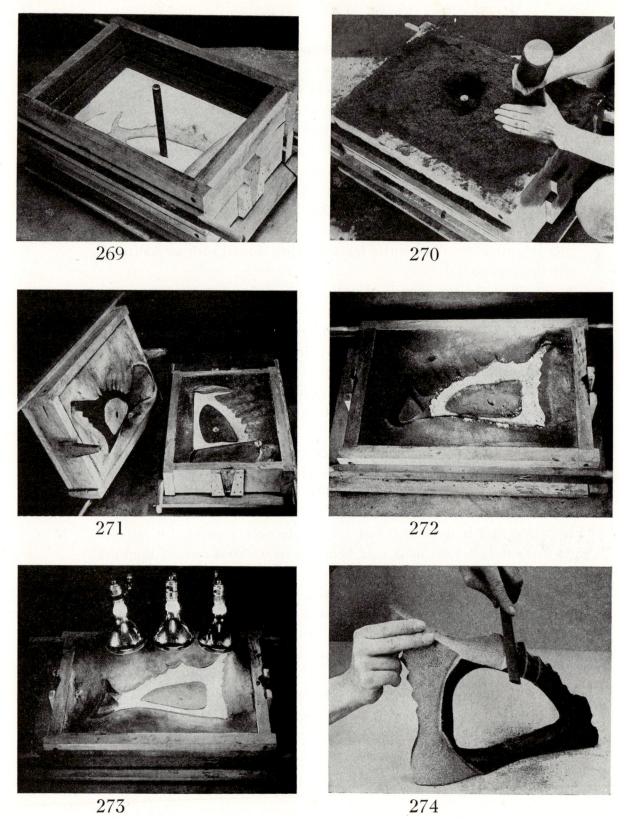

269

270

271

272

273

274

Methods of Coring

Cores for hollow castings are made by several methods, depending on the type of object being cast. Sharp sand is mixed with linseed oil and pressed into a special core mold or into the sand mold itself after removing the model. It must be baked at 450° F for about one hour to harden it and drive off gases from the oil. If it is cast directly in the sand mold, the entire assembly must be baked and the core removed and shaved down to allow space for the metal to flow. A plaster mold of the model could be made and used for a core box, as this kind of mold is called. Another method is to use molding sand for the core and build it up around a strong armature inside the sand mold. In this latter case the sand is adhesive enough to hold itself together with the aid of the armature and no core box is needed for baking.

A simple and direct method of making a core is shown in Figures 272 and 273. The shape of the form is such that part of it does not need a core, being only about ½ inch thick. The small piece enclosing a portion of the thicker section of the mold is replaced on the drag. Graphite is dusted over the inside of the mold and the core sand mixture is pressed firmly into the drag (Figure 272). The core is overbuilt slightly and the cope carefully replaced on the drag, giving a reasonably accurate impression to the core sand. The cope is removed and a series of infra-red heat lamps are used to partially volatilize the oil in the sand, so that the core will be sturdy enough to lift from the mold (Figure 273). Any radiant heat, such as the broiler used in melting wax or an inverted hot plate, will also serve this purpose. If the core is more than an inch thick, it should be heated in two stages: first, when a layer about ½ inch thick has been pressed into the drag and again after the shaping of the core is completed.

As the core is being heated, moisture will be taken out of the surrounding molding sand. Brushing the surface periodically with molasses water will help prevent cracking. The best indication of sufficient heating is a slight darkening of the surface of the core. It should not be overheated and the heat source should be far enough from the sand so that it penetrates into the core before burning the surface. The core will gain in strength as it cools.

243

When the core is hard, it is lifted carefully from the mold and placed in a bed of molding sand to help support its weight and baked at 450° F for an hour. After cooling, the core is strong enough to handle freely and a layer the thickness of the eventual cast (¼ inch) is systematically filed off as shown in Figure 274.

At the bottom of the sprue, a reservoir is scooped out of the sand with a molding tool and gates are cut which will channel the metal into the mold. The core is anchored inside the drag by using metal spacers called chaplets (Figure 275). A funnel is cut into the cope at the top of the sprue, and a long wire is pushed through the sand a number of times to help vent the gases from the metal. After checking to see that the core and pieces are properly placed, the cope is replaced on the drag and the mold is ready to pour (Figure 276).

It can easily be seen that coring complicates the sand molding process considerably. Often, the amount of metal saved and the weight eliminated are completely off-set by the difficulty of making a core. This is especially true when casting in aluminum which is so light that only a large core could make an appreciable saving in weight. Small sculptures, or ones with sections an inch or less in thickness, usually should not be cored regardless of the kind of metal being poured. The piece used in this demonstration could very well have been cast solid, since its heaviest part is only slightly over one inch in thickness. The coring procedure was carried out here primarily for the sake of illustration.

275

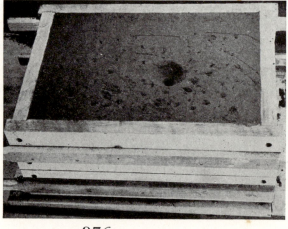

276

Cast Iron

Cast iron has many possibilities for some types of sculpture. Its coarse grain and brittleness are definite limitations and demand a broadness and bigness of concept. Compared to bronze, cast iron suggests something of the difference one finds between wood and stone. The iron is cold, formidable, and heavy; forms designed for it must reflect these characteristics.

The melting point of cast iron is 2065° F to 2400° F and the pouring temperature between 2600° F and 2850° F, which is much higher than that of bronze. Usually, a reverberatory furnace or a cupola is used for melting. In the former the heat is deflected downward to the surface of the metal and the molten metal is drained off from the bottom. In a cupola, which is a kind of blast furnace, the metal is melted in direct contact with the fuel. Iron can be melted in the same furnace that is used for the nonferrous metals but, of course, more time is necessary to build up the required heat. The same silicon carbide crucibles used in melting brass and bronze are also used for gray iron.

Cast iron owes its excellent casting qualities to its high carbon content which ranges from 2 to 4 percent, and to its relatively small shrinkage.

When the iron has been poured and allowed to cool for about half an hour, the mold can be dumped by lifting the cope and shaking the sand out of the flask. The cast, still very hot but not fragile, can be picked up with hand tongs and placed on top of the sand so as to cool more quickly. Cast iron is quite brittle and much less malleable than brass and bronze. The gates should be broken off by a sharp blow with a heavy hammer, being sure that no thin section of the casting is strained in the process. Chasing is best done by using a high-speed silicon carbide grind wheel to cut through the hard skin and then by finishing the area with files. The iron can be polished by rubbing with steel wool and coating the surface immediately with wax. Colors ranging from bright orange to dark brown can be obtained simply by causing the metal to rust. Dilute nitric acid, lime paste, or salt water

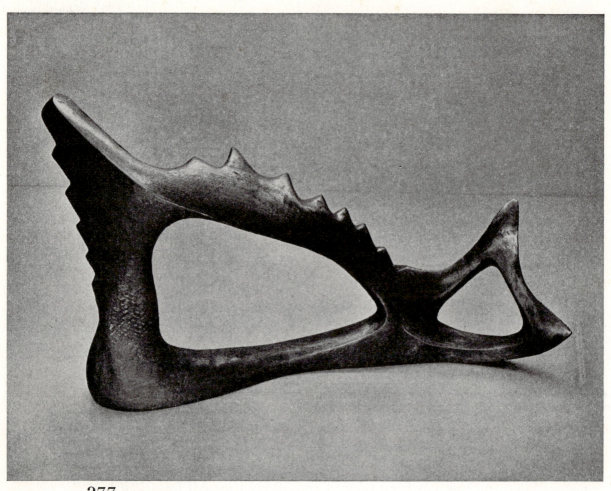

277

will speed up the oxidation, and when the desired color is reached, the cast can be covered with a thin coat of lacquer or wax.

The cast from our demonstration mold (Figure 277) is polished in some areas and colored in others. The hard cold quality of the metal is reflected in the character of the form.

18· Summary

IN THE preceding chapters, a few ideas have been discussed in detail, others only in general terms, and some only implied. Often, many words were needed to explain a point of lesser importance than the effort indicated. More essential statements, sometimes expressed in fewer words, may have caught less of the reader's attention because of their brevity. Wherever possible, an attempt has been made to establish the relative value of ideas as they were presented. A summary will be helpful to review, assimilate, and possibly re-evaluate the basic principles of the foregoing chapters.

Of the three elements of sculpture—idea, form, and technical means—the third has occupied the most space in this book. This does not imply that the other two are of lesser importance. There can be no hierarchy of value among the three; one cannot exist, sculpturally, without the others. True, there may be varying degrees of emphasis placed on them, but this does not make one more essential. An idea which is badly designed and mishandled technically cannot result in a successful visual expression no matter how important the thought behind it. On the other hand, craftsmanship is empty unless one has something to say through a visual form. The sculptor is the speaker, the material is the language, and the technique is the voice; what is said is the form. Form, content, and material comprise the unit which is the sculpture. The material-form is the concept; there is no sculptural meaning apart from it. If the material-form fails to express the original concept, we cannot say it is a good concept poorly expressed, since sculpture can only be judged visually. In other words, the ability to express a concept visually should be implicit in that concept itself. Perhaps only a small portion of it is consciously conceived, but the form may be full blown in the subconscious before the physical construction is started. As a sculptor "works out" a form, he is, at least to some extent, simply becoming conscious of solutions already resolved in his subconscious mind. Of course, there are unforeseen problems, trials and errors, and sudden inspirations, but he recognizes solutions and feels confidence in them only to the degree that the concept was preconceived, whether consciously or unconsciously.

A sculpture can never transcend its maker. It is his expression and is controlled by what he has to express. The sculptor's knowledge, experience, and capacities are, then, the over-all control, the ultimate factors in the value of the work. But having something to say, alone, does not make one a sculptor; the value of the ideas can be realized only when synthesized into visual expression. One cannot be taught how to produce a work of art, but one can learn to make use of the potentials of materials, techniques, and design, and thereby release whatever creative capacity one has. The creative imagination can be stimulated and encouraged to grow through repetition of the creative process.

Creative concepts often grow out of vague, half-understood feelings, attitudes, and ideas. Sculpture is not a mystery; it more nearly the answer to a mystery. The sculptor, in his attempt to make real his abstract concepts, actualizes them in space. He tries to make the elusive thought-image as real as the material in which it is done. He brings into being his concepts of existence and his feeling for order. Often he chooses a simple and seemingly insignificant subject through which his concept flows. He may glorify or protest or make his statement calmly. Being tantalizingly close to divinity himself, he wants more than nature has given him. He wants to understand more than his mind can

248

comprehend and to see more than his eyes can see. Unable to grasp the complexity of nature, he wants to create man's world—one that he can understand and share with his fellow men. He seeks forms that are essential in his terms, not nature's. But wisely he realizes that the laws of nature are also his laws and that he does well to study her system and her laws.

Art is not primarily an intellectual process, at least not in the usual sense of the word. It has not grown from a crude beginning to a highly developed stage as have some of our sciences. The great value of art is that it goes beyond our powers of rationalization. It has always sprung from man's deeper feelings about his universe and not from his factual knowledge. Art comes through convictions; one is not convinced by facts but through feeling. Artistically, factual knowledge has value to the extent that it develops our sensitivity and emotional energy. If such knowledge does not grow into a broader understanding of life, it becomes an obstacle, interfering with the development of our convictions.

Primitive sculptors had a direct and intuitive approach to form. We can learn much from studying their sculptures, particularly if we understand some of the concepts behind them. For instance, most of their forms were fetishes, some of which were carried on the body as protection. The sculptor did not represent the god in a certain material; the material became the god-form. It was as real as himself, or perhaps more real. If we can find in our own beliefs a similar kind of realness—a direct approach to form problems—we will have a firm basis for our sculpture. We cannot imitate the primitive; our concepts are different from theirs. But our sculptural problems of material and form are the same, and their solutions may help us to find our own.

We can learn much about design from the manner in which the primitive sculptors brought their concepts into being. Design is not an afterthought, added to a form to make it more pleasing; it is not frosting on a cake. The design is the totality of the shape relationships. In other words, it is the form-concept, and can be separated from idea and material only in theoretical terms. Design is the spatial organization that makes a mass one and the same thing from all views. There can be no sculptural concept without this three-dimensional

249

oneness. Design does more; it stimulates the visual perception beyond the normal seeing process. It anticipates what is yet to be seen, one view leading to the next. By clearly defining dimensions, it presents a stronger visual perception of space and form in space than we are accustomed to seeing. And finally, through its organizational structure it expresses the content of the sculpture. In nearly all primitive periods, even though widely separated geographically and chronologically, we find design performing these functions. The primitive sculptors, like all great sculptors, gave their abstract concepts a visual life and a spatial realness through formal organization. The vitality of their simplified forms reflects their firm convictions and mastery of craftsmanship.

The materials and techniques discussed in this book are presented in sufficient detail to give a student a working knowledge of the various processes. However, they were chosen more for their contribution to the creative process than as a general technical survey. There are materials and techniques other than these with as great a creative potential; but the ones included cover most of the technical problems encountered in sculpture, and when one has learned a few methods well, others can be learned quickly.

As we have seen, certain principles apply to all materials and techniques. First, the sculptural potential of the material has to be understood. Then, techniques for using this potential must be found. Each material will have certain possibilities and limitations in terms of a particular technique; another technique may allow exploitation of different aspects of the material. In other words, regardless of the sculptural potential of a material, the sculptor is limited to his technical knowledge of handling it. Very often what is called a limitation of the material is a limitation of the technique. Clay is just so much shapeless, pliable substance until a modeling technique is applied to it; a block of wood is only an arbitrary mass until its inherent life is released by controlled carving.

It is possible to know all the scientific facts about a material and still have no feeling for it. On the other hand, one may have an intuitive understanding of the substance without knowing the molecular structure or the physical, biological, and chemical processes involved in its development. These scientific facts may help in understanding the nature of a material and are of particular advantage in the controlling of material through various techniques, but one must not become so interested in factual knowledge as to forget the real purpose of learning about materials and techniques.

Technical means, like words, should be learned thoroughly enough so that we can think with them. Just as our verbal thinking is limited to our vocabulary, visual conception is limited by the ability to handle materials. Knowing about a technique is not of value in itself; the knowledge must be understood and assimilated into the creative thinking processes. If one understands the nature of molten metal and the means of directing its flow, more possibilities of metal form are available to the creative imagination than if one knows only the cold-working techniques of cutting, bending, hammering, etc. Then, in the visualization of form, the mind is not only freed from the curbs of technical inability, but this understanding and feeling for the process stimulates the imagination. Forms may be visualized that were impossible to conceive without this knowledge. But if the technique is only half learned, if one has to struggle with it mentally, it will be a handicap in the creative process. When the meanings of words are vague in our minds, thinking with these words is necessarily vague, and we would do better to formulate our thoughts in simpler, well-understood terms. The same is true of technical knowledge; unless it is clear enough not to interfere with the process of creative visualization, one will do better to think through other means for which one has a feeling.

One gains from experience what one puts into it. A limited vocabulary, whether verbal or visual, limits one's reactions by not allowing fine shades of difference in meaning. On seeing the Grand Canyon a man may simply say it is big because that is the only word he has to describe his feelings; and, though sensing it is not quite the right term, he lumps this experience in with others which were quite different. If one studies nature with the purpose of understanding its formal structure, then one can expect to profit by the effort in proportion to one's capacity for thinking in formal terms. Technical knowledge alone is not enough, but in so far as it frees the imagination and is assimilated in the creative thinking process, it is vital.

251

The amount of technical knowledge a sculptor has does not determine his ability as a sculptor. Great sculpture can be created with the simplest of techniques and materials. If the sculptor knows only one material and one way of handling it, he may be limited in his conception of form, but if he knows this one material and technique well and can think through it, he will be better off, sculpturally, than one who has only a vague knowledge of many technical means. How many materials and techniques a sculptor attempts to master is a personal problem. Some may find only a few necessary for their expressions, others may want to learn as many as possible. Any student should learn a simple technique well and experience its synthesis with the creative process before becoming involved in new ones. He should learn, not formulas, but basic principles. It is impossible for a student to gain the experience necessary to call himself a sculptor in the short time usually alloted for study. A firm foundation of basic principles, a general direction, and an understanding of how to continue learning is the most he can expect. His individual development is in his own hands; he may be encouraged to find his own convictions, but they cannot be handed to him.

Studying the work of other sculptors, contemporary as well as historical, is of great importance. Sculpture is a universal and timeless language. Since the beginning, sculptors have had the problems of form similar to those that confront us. Philosophical beliefs and sociological conditions have changed, but man's attempt to express himself sculpturally remains a problem of form in space.

We are living in a rational age, believing that reality is verifiable. We demand physical facts, not feelings, for our beliefs. We are proud of our ability to control nature, even though sometimes we may forget that we ourselves are a part of it. We are aware of our lack of convictions and continually search for that in which we can firmly believe. We envy the naïveté of children and admire the work of primitive artists, yet our minds cannot cast off the weight of factual knowledge. We cannot simply stop being self-conscious. To try to escape society, to ignore that which confronts us every day, is impossible. Attempts to evade the issue or to backtrack only add to the confusion.

At least part of the answer to this dilemma lies in ourselves. We still have the capacity for feeling and for developing convictions. The need for them and the expression of them is vital in our whole make-up. But we are not sufficiently critical of our standards of value. Too often we accept without feeling, or discard a tradition without ever having understood it. We look for formulas rather than principles. We borrow ideas and voice words that have no real meaning to us. We have made ourselves nearsighted in our visualization.

The sculptor in this complex civilization has basically the same problems as his predecessors. He must find his own answers eventually, making use of whatever help he can find in their sculpture, but not arbitrarily adopting their forms and techniques. He cannot ignore contemporary technical knowledge; to do so would defy tradition as well as progress itself. His work must become a normal part of his life and a normal part of his expression.

Sculpture is not something that we decide to have or not to have. It is implicit in our lives. Its place in our scale of values may be lowered; we may misunderstand its purpose, or seek its kind of expression in other kinds of forms. We may insist that it serve some more utilitarian purpose, such as a lamp or a tie pin. We may at times be content to study cloud forms or collect pebbles on the beach, without realizing that we are looking for the kind of expression that sculpture affords. But regardless of the unawareness or distortion of its purpose and meaning, we can be sure that sculpture is a vital part of life as long as children instinctively make mud pies. It is up to us to clarify our conception of this need and to establish means of satisfying it.

Of course, we can live physically without any of the arts. We know from scientific investigations just what is necessary to sustain life on a mechanical level, and art is not included. However, to a human being, living is more than animal existence. To think abstractly and to demand expression of our thoughts is what distinguishes us from other animals.

APPENDIX 1

Suggestions for Further Reading

The following list of readings is divided into two groups: those that deal specifically with the problems covered in individual chapters and those that cover certain aspects of the book but do not refer directly to any one chapter. Rather than divide the latter into small parts which could be related to separate chapters, they are left intact and suggested as general references.

Chapter 1

Hudnut, Joseph: *Modern Sculpture,* W. W. Norton & Co., New York, 1929

Wilenski, R. H.: *The Meaning of Modern Sculpture,* Parts I and II, Frederick A. Stokes Co., New York, 1935

Chapter 2

Scott, Robert G.: *Design Fundamentals,* McGraw-Hill Book Co., New York, 1951

Hildebrand, Adolf: *Problem of Form,* Chapters I, II, and III, G. E. Stechert & Co., New York, 1907

Wilenski, R. H.: *The Meaning of Modern Sculpture,* Part III, Frederick A. Stokes Co., New York, 1935

Chapter 3

Jagger, Sargeant: *Modelling and Sculpture in the Making,* Studio, London, 1933

Chapter 4

Wilenski, R. H.: *The Meaning of Modern Sculpture,* Parts IV and V, Frederick A. Stokes Co., New York, 1935

Chapter 6

Martin, J. L., Nicholson, B., and Gabo, N., editors: *Circle,* editorial by N. Gabo, "The Constructive Idea in Art," pages 1-10, and Section II, "Sculpture," pages 77-129. E. Weyhe, New York (undated)

Moholy-Nagy, L.: *Vision in Motion,* Chapter on Sculpture, Paul Theobald, Chicago, 1947

Read, Herbert; Olson, Ruth; Chanin, Abraham: *Gabo-Pevsner,* Museum of Modern Art, New York, 1948

Sweeney, James J.: *Alexander Calder,* Museum of Modern Art, New York, 1943

de Kooning, Elaine: "David Smith Makes a Sculpture" in *Art News,* Vol. 50, No. 5, September 1951

Chapter 7

Nicolaides, Kimon: *The Natural Way to Draw,* Houghton Mifflin Co., Boston, 1941

Chapter 8

Walters, Carl: "Ceramic Sculpture, Tools and Materials" in *American Magazine of Art,* Vol. 28, pages 500-502, 561-563, August and September 1935

Snively, R. D., and Snively, M. E.: *Pottery,* Stephen Daye Press, Brattleboro, Vt., 1940

Meyer, Joan F.: "Thrown Ceramic Sculpture" in *Craft Horizons,* Vol. IX, No. 2, New York, 1949

Chapter 9

Miller, Alec: *Stone and Marble Carving,* University of Calif. Press, Berkeley and Los Angeles, 1948

Gill, Eric: *An Essay on Stone Cutting*, St. Dominic's Press, Ditchling, Sussex, 1924

Chapter 10

Rood, John: *Sculpture in Wood*, University of Minnesota Press, Minneapolis, 1950

Durst, Alan: *Wood Carving*, Studio, London, 1928

Sweeney, James J.: *Henry Moore*, Simon and Schuster, New York, 1946

Chapter 11

Hildebrand, Adolf: *Problem of Form*, Chapters III, IV, and V, G. E. Stechert & Co., New York, 1907

Chapter 14

Clarke, Carl D.: *Molding and Casting*, Standard Arts Press, Baltimore, 1946

Chapter 15

Fingesten, P.: "Sculpture in Cement" in *American Artist*, Vol. 7, pages 22-23, 16-17, January and February 1943

Plastic Magnesia Cements, Dow Chemical Co., Midland, Mich.

Seaton, Max: "Plastic Magnesite and Oxychloride Cement" in *Chemical and Metallurgical Engineering*, Vol. 25, New York, 1921

Chapter 16

Johnson, R. W.: "The Practice of Direct Casting" in *Technical Studies*, Fogg Art Museum, Harvard University, Vol. VIII, No. 4, April 1940

Johnson, R. W.: "The Direct Casting of Figures" in *Technical Studies*, Fogg Art Museum, Harvard University, Vol. IX, No. 4, April 1941

Lenz, Hugh H.: *The Alfred David Lenz System of Lost Wax Casting*, National Sculpture Society, New York, 1933

Clarke, Carl D.: *Metal Casting of Sculpture*, Standard Arts Press, Butler, Md., 1948

Underwood, Leon: *Bronzes of West Africa*, Alec Tiranti, London, 1949

Master Bronzes, Albright Art Gallery, Buffalo, New York, 1937

General References

Seymour, Charles: *Tradition and Experiment in Modern Sculpture*, American University Press, Washington, 1949

Valentiner, W. R.: *Origins of Modern Sculpture*, Wittenborn, New York, 1946

Faulkner, R., Ziegfeld, E., and Hill, G.: *Art Today*, Chapter on Sculpture, Henry Holt & Co., New York, rev. ed., 1949

Rindge, A. M.: *Sculpture*, Harcourt, Brace & Co., New York, 1929

Giedieon-Welcker, C.: *Modern Plastic Art*, Dr. H. Girsberger, Zurich, 1937

Ferguson, Duncan: "Clay Modelling in the Round" in *American Magazine of Art*, Vol. 28, No. 1, January 1935

Ferguson, Duncan: "Relief in Clay, Modelling in Wax, Modelling in Plaster, Casting" in *American Magazine of Art*, Vol. 28, No. 2, February 1935

Zorach, William: *Zorach Explains Sculpture*, American Artists Group, New York, 1947

Slobodkin, Louis: *Sculpture, Principles and Practice*, World Publishing Co., Cleveland, 1949

Rich, Jack C.: *The Materials and Methods of Sculpture*, Oxford University Press, New York, 1947

Hoffman, Malvina: *Sculpture, Inside and Out*, W. W. Norton & Co., New York, 1939

Some Sources of Supply of Tools and Materials

The numbers following these items indicate the companies listed on the next page which sell them. The order of the numbers is incidental and does not imply recommendations.

Cast Stone
calcium chloride 1
hydrometers 2
Hydrostone 1, 53
Keene's cement 1, 53
magnesium chloride 46
magnesium oxide 46
Mapico colors 13
marble chips 1, 4
Perlite 1, 6
Portland cement 1
stainless steel 35, 39, 56
terra cotta aggregate 1, 4
Thermo-con cellular concrete 29

Clay Modeling
aluminum armature wire 3, 35, 39, 56
armatures 24, 47, 48, 50
ball clay 20, 26, 49, 50
barium carbonate 2, 18, 20, 26
grog (brick dust) 1, 7, 18, 20, 25
kilns 7, 14, 18, 20, 25, 41, 50
low-fire colored clays 7
manganese dioxide 2, 20, 26
modeling stands 24, 25, 48, 50
modeling tools 5, 7, 24, 25, 47, 48, 50
Ohio shale (red clay) 7, 18, 20, 27, 50
plasteline 7, 10, 24, 25, 47, 48, 50
potter's wheels 7, 18, 20, 25, 50
red iron oxide 2, 3, 20, 26
wedging boards 7, 25

Flexible Molding Material
alum 2, 10
carbolic acid 2, 22
Cold Molding Compound 40
Elastomer (105) 23
formaldehyde 2, 22
gelatin 10, 22, 24, 48, 50
glycerin 2, 10, 22
Koroseal FMC 40
latex liquid rubber 17, 24, 47, 48, 50

sorbital 9
toluene 2, 22
zinc sulphate 2, 22

Metal: Construction and Casting
aluminum 14, 35, 39, 56
brass 14, 35, 39, 56
bronze 35, 39, 56
Cerrobend 35
chemicals 2, 10, 22
copper 14, 35, 39, 56
core oil 11
crucibles 11, 30, 45
flux 11
ingot metal 8, 35, 39, 56
lead sheets 3, 14, 35, 39, 56
melting furnaces 16, 45, 57
metal working tools 14
Modalloy 51
molding sand 11, 30
Non-Ferrous Investment 53
phosphor-copper 8
pneumatic chipping hammer 3, 14
pouring shanks 11, 30, 45
silica flour 1, 11, 30
solder 3, 35, 39, 56
stainless steel 35, 39, 56
talc 18, 26, 27
tongs 11, 30, 45
torches (gas) 3, 14
waxes 2, 3, 10, 22, 45 (see *Wax*)
zinc 8, 14

Plaster: Building, Molding, and Casting
alcohol 2, 3
armature wire 3, 35, 39, 56
burlap 10, 24, 48, 50
carbon tetrachloride 2, 3
cold rolled steel 3, 14
dextrin 10
green soap 2, 10, 22
hemp fiber (jute) 10
Hydrocal 1, 53
Hydrostone 1, 53
mixing bowls 24, 47, 48, 50
molding plaster 1, 53
Non-Ferrous Investment 53
plaster tools 5, 7, 10, 24, 25, 34, 47, 48, 50

rasps 3, 5, 14, 24, 25, 47, 48, 50
shellac 3, 10
shim brass 3, 24, 35, 39, 47, 48, 50, 56
stearin 10, 22

Plastics: Construction and Casting
Lucite sheets and rods 14, 21, 43
phenolic resin 33
Plexiglas sheets and rods 14, 43, 44
polyester resin 42

Stone Carving
air compressors 3, 16, 19
air hose 3, 19, 28
air regulators 3, 19
hand tools 3, 10, 15, 24, 47, 48, 50
limestone 4, 12, 31, 32
marble 4, 37, 52, 54
pneumatic tools 15, 28
putty powder 3, 10
rasps 3, 10, 15, 24, 47, 48, 50
waterproof sandpaper 3, 10, 14

Wax
beeswax 3, 10
carnauba wax 10, 45
microcrystalline wax 45
paraffin 2, 3, 10, 45
rosin 2, 3, 10, 45
stearin 10, 22
vaseline 2

Wood: Construction and Carving
hardwoods 14, 36, 38, 47, 55
plywood 1, 14
rasps 3, 7, 24, 34, 47, 48, 50
sharpening stones 3, 47
softwoods 1, 14
wood carving tables 14
wood carving tools 24, 34, 47, 48, 50
wood carving vises 3, 14
workshop tools (hand and machine) 3, 14

1. Local building supply companies
2. Local chemical supply companies
3. Local hardware companies
4. Local stone yards or monument companies
5. Adams, Henry, 28 Locust Place, Great Kills, Staten Island 8, N. Y.
6. Alatex Construction Service, 3518 Broadway, New Orleans 18, La.
7. American Art Clay Co., 4717 West 16th St., Indianapolis 24, Ind.
8. American Smelting & Refining Co., Fed. Metals Div., 120 Broadway, New York 5, N. Y.
9. Atlas Powder Co., Wilmington 99, Del.
10. Behlen & Brothers, Inc., 10 Christopher St., New York 14, N. Y.
11. Bell, M. A., Co., St. Louis 2, Mo.
12. Bloomington Limestone Corp., 110 East 42d St., New York 17, N. Y.
13. Binney & Smith, 41 East 42d St., New York 17, N. Y.
14. Brodhead-Garrett Co., Cleveland 5, Ohio.
15. Brunner & Lay, 727-739 South Jefferson St., Chicago, Ill.
16. Campbell-Hausfeld Co., Harrison, Ohio
17. Cementex Co., Inc., 336 Canal St., New York 13, N. Y.
18. Denver Fire Clay Co., Denver, Colo.
19. Devilbiss Co., Toledo 1, Ohio
20. Drakenfeld & Co., 45-47 Park Place, New York 7, N. Y.
21. Du Pont de Nemours, E. I., & Co., Arlington, N. J.
22. Eimer & Amend, 635 Greenwich St., New York 14, N. Y.
23. Elastomer Chemical Corp, 113 East Centre St., Nutley 10, N. J.
24. Ettl Studios, 213 West 58th St., New York 19, N. Y.
25. Favor, Ruhl & Co., 425 South Wabash Ave., Chicago 5, Ill.
26. Ferro Enamel Corp., 4150 East 15th St., Cleveland 5, Ohio
27. George Fetzer & Co., 1205 17th Ave., Cleveland 11, Ohio
28. Granite City Tool Co., Barre, Vt.
29. Higgins Inc., New Orleans 22, La.
30. Hill & Griffith Co., Birmingham 1, Ala.
31. Indian Hill Stone Co., Bloomington, Ind.
32. Indiana Limestone Co., N. Y., 40 East 41st St., New York 17, N. Y.
33. Marblette Corp., 37-21 30th St., Long Island City 1, N. Y.
34. Martini, M., 319 East 61st St., New York 21, N. Y.
35. Metal Goods Corp., 5239 Brown Ave., St. Louis, Mo.
36. Monteath, J. H., Co., 2500 Park Ave., Bronx 51, N. Y.
37. Musto-Keenan Co., 525 N. Point St., San Francisco, Calif.
38. Overseas Trading Co., 422 Natchez St., New Orleans 12, La.
39. Pacific Metals Co., 3100 19th St., San Francisco, Calif.
40. Perma-Flex Mold Co., 1919 East Livingston Ave., Columbus 9, Ohio
41. Petterson Kilns, 1007 S. Acacia St., Compton, Calif.
42. Pittsburgh Plate Glass Co., Grant Bldg., Pittsburgh 19, Pa.
43. Plastic Supply Co., 2901 N. Grand Blvd., St. Louis 7, Mo.
44. Rohm & Haas Co., Philadelphia 5, Pa.
45. Saunders, Alexander, & Co., 95 Bedford St., New York 14, N. Y.
46. Schundler, F. E., & Co., 504 Railroad St., Joliet, Ill.
47. Sculpture Associates, 114 St. Marks Place, New York 3, N. Y.
48. Sculpture House, 304 West 42d St., New York 18, N. Y.
49. Spinks, H. C., Clay Co., 1103 First National Bank Bldg., Cincinnati 2, Ohio
50. Stewart Clay Co., 629-33 East 16th St., New York 9, N. Y.
51. Studio Supply Co., 23 Judge St., Brooklyn 11, N. Y.
52. Trani Marble & Tile Works, 437 East 23d St., New York 10, N. Y.
53. U. S. Gypsum Co., 300 West Adams St., Chicago 6, Ill.
54. Vermont Marble Co., 101 Park Ave., New York 17, N. Y.
55. White Brothers, 5th and Brannon Sts., San Francisco, Calif.
56. Whitehead Metal Products Co., 303 West 10th St., New York 11, N. Y.
57. Whiting Corp., Harvey, Ill.